Not Just Footy

Also by George Huitker

An Unfamiliar Sea
The Actor Is Happy
An Unfamiliar Actor
How To Succeed Without Really Winning

Not Just Footy
George Huitker

Not Just Footy
ISBN 978 1 74027 085 4
Copyright © George Huitker 2007

First published 2001
Published 2007 with minor revisions by
GINNINDERRA PRESS
PO Box 6753 Charnwood ACT 2615
www.ginninderrapress.com.au

Printed by Pirion Digital, Fyshwick, ACT

Contents

For Jeane,
proprietor of the best sideline canteen operation
the world has known,

for Sue,
for helping me to understand the value of nurture,

for the Radford Bill Turner squad of 2001,
for not allowing me to finish this story off,

and for all the players I've coached or played alongside.

I truly am sorry.

'Talent is overrated,' Ted told me.
'That you're not very talented needn't be the end of it.'
– Ted Seabrooke in John Irving's *The Imaginary Girlfriend, A Memoir*, 1996

'A major problem in Western culture...is how to channel young men's natural aggression now that war and hunting are obsolete. Sports sop up some of it.'
– Margaret Wente, *Counterpoint*, 2000

'Better to win by admitting your sin than to lose with a halo.'
– Eva Peron in Andrew Lloyd Webber's *Evita*, 1976

Not Just a Foreword

The French philosopher Albert Camus once famously wrote, 'All that I know about life I learnt from football.'

Camus was once a player. Not a particularly good one but an active player none the less. And that makes him pretty much like most of us. If there are an estimated two billion fans of football (a game played with the foot and where the aim is to manipulate a spherical ball) on the planet, the odds are good that whoever reads this book did at one time play the game.

Which is just as well. To understand the real essence of the football thing, it is at least helpful to have played it. And then, of course, as a natural progression, watched it and maybe even coached it.

All of the above can mirror the kaleidoscope of life itself. To be picked in your first team, or to be taken to your first game, is like the miracle of birth. To score your first goal is nearly as gratifying as consummating your first love affair. And to see your team lose, whether as a player or a supporter, is to look death square in the face.

Which is what makes football so difficult to define. Some stuffed tracksuit in America once said, 'In sport winning is not everything. It's the only thing.' Well, not so in football.

In this sport, fidelity is for the most part maintained, win, lose or draw. A fan, who recently watched his beloved team suffer an interminable string of defeats, explained, 'It's a real hard slog supporting these boys. But it helps develop mental toughness, builds character and gives you a bloody good laugh.'

Football is life and, as George Huitker says, not just footy. Huitker as a fan, a son of a fan, a player and a coach – narrates a classic every-man football story. The highs, the lows, the joys, the frustrations, the rewards and the ingratitude are all there in ways and doses we can recognise all too well. We have all played this game.

Albert Camus fancied the ideal that the world is one brotherhood. He saw humanity as one large club in which all players pull together in struggle and friendship.

He really must have played football, too.

Les Murray

Not Just a Second Foreword

The life of a human being is so vast and unique that at times I find it hard to completely comprehend – in a positive way – why mine has pretty much been based around a simple game known as football.

So far in my life voyage I have dedicated myself to this game for twelve years out of the eighteen that I have lived. Obviously, the dedication has intensified over the years. However, the passion and energy I possess for football has been as strong from the days I played one-on-one with Dad in the living room during childhood to when I captained my country at Under 17 level in the Youth World Cup in Peru in 2005. As a footballer or, as I like to call myself, 'an aspiring professional footballer', you tend to lead a pretty unpredictable lifestyle which varies regularly as you are faced with differing challenges on a daily basis. One day you can feel alone and doubtful, whereas the next day you feel as if you are on top of the world. It is a lifestyle of constant and changing experiences which has already provided me with a knowledge and understanding far beyond the actual game itself. There is so much more to it all than the ninety-minute games we all watch on weekends.

Over many decades, football has undoubtedly created a unique worldwide intrigue that has spread throughout the globe. It is an intrigue that has created not only a major stage to showcase some of the most unbelievably skilled athletes in the world, but also its own distinct and universal culture. In some places it has almost become the equivalent to a religion. Just think about the number of die-hard fans across the globe who may not be training throughout the week or even playing football on the weekends, but in their own way have dedicated themselves to this game simply through supporting a team. I cannot help but wonder at how such a simple game can become the sole inspiration of one's life, as is the case with my own.

Growing up in Canberra I was infused with a love for football. I not only enjoyed it but I thrived upon that feeling of dancing with that ball, no matter what the conditions. I was never completely aware of the inspiration it initially gave me. Yet football is something that has always been a part of me, not something that has been instilled – and I believe there is a fine distinction. I like to think that I have *dedicated* my whole childhood to this game, not sacrificed it. The people who are closest to me are the ones who have made sacrifices. My father coached me throughout all my childhood years, not only on Saturday game day or weekdays with the team, but in the house after he finished work each day. I would practise new tricks after school in the hope of gaining a reaction from him when he returned (which I think many other children do during a similar stage in their lives). To hear him say 'Well done!' or to see that impressed smile on his face brought me so much joy and self confidence. And during actual matches I always found a hidden energy to do more when my dad was watching, even to this day.

During the time I first entered into the representative teams of the ACT, I distinctly remember the politics that surrounded my taking part. When I think back to those days, I thank my father for never getting involved in the political aspect. He shared his passion of the game with myself and my team-mates in more positive ways: coaching, managing and even creating his own special tactical coaches manual. On occasions there would be other parents conspiring against my abilities, as well as my love and dedication to the game. When I was fast-tracked up an age group in representative sides or academies we would hear rumours of my father's involvement on some sort of selection panel. But when I come to think about this now, I realise my father actually *was* involved in my advancement into higher divisions and representative teams in that he sacrificed his time to coach, babysit, organise and support not only me but also many other young players. He created coaching drills and printed various copies for younger coaches and he revolutionised the pee-wee program at my childhood club – all voluntarily. I think those parents who just sat and watched and made you feel uncomfortable because their son wasn't being selected were absolutely correct: I was fast-tracked and successful *because* of my father's practical rather than political involvement with my teams in the sport I loved.

I firmly believe that I would not be where I am today if it wasn't for the time not only my dad but my whole family invested in me. With unfaltering, positive support from the people surrounding you - and through their belief in you – it is amazing what you can achieve. I can recall that in times of immense self doubt my family provided me with a solid backbone, making it possible to stand straight and tall and simply *enjoy* what I was doing. A fine example was at my first national titles representing the ACT at Under 14 level. We faced NSW Country in our opening match and were humiliated by five goals to nothing. I remember how much I had individually prepared for this tournament and also how hard we had worked as a team in the lead up. While we were aware of NSW's reputation, to lose 5–0 in your first national title match really made it feel as if this was as far as we were ever going to get to in terms of football. I cried that night on the phone to my father trying my hardest to explain to him that the opposing players were freaks and that I couldn't match them at all. I was fed up because I thought that I wasn't good enough. But my Dad just kept laughing it off. The following morning we were up against Northern NSW and to be honest, my spirits were not at their highest. Just before we walked out onto the pitch Dad came over to me and even though I gave him a stubbornly despondent face, what he had to say to me instantly changed my whole outlook right there and then. I will never forget his words: 'Kaz, it's only a game, such a simple one at that. Just play how you know best. Dance with the ball and don't worry so much.' We were eventual victors by 2 goals to 1.

Following that match, my parents were approached by a player agent who had been genuinely interested in what I had exhibited on the field during that game. It had all happened so quickly. Not even twenty-four hours had passed since my seemingly serious self doubts had first manifested themselves. It amazes me now how frequently these sort of occurrences and swift changes can take place in the world of football, presenting the players involved with an opportunity to not only capitalise and re-invent themselves on the field but to experience and understand how powerful both the human mind and a belief in oneself can really be. Almost a year following the national titles and meeting with the agent that day, I found myself in Spain training with Real Madrid in their Cadete A junior team. At age fourteen, this was my first taste of European football and it was something that I had only ever dreamed about. I was in a different world there in

Madrid. Through the strong Spanish football culture, I witnessed and felt so much of what the game had to offer. And I had forgotten all about my self-doubt. In the two weeks I spent there I was instantly hooked. The greatest part about my experience in Spain was that my dad was there by my side, providing me with the belief that one day, if it was what I wanted, this sort of life was possible.

It is only on rare occasions that you actually get to sit back and completely digest what is occurring to you in the life you lead as an aspiring professional footballer. It is both physically and psychologically demanding as you are continually forced to deal with all sorts of differing situations and challenges that are placed in front of you. At times you can feel immensely drained or unbelievably rewarded. And half the time, you are competing'one-on-one against your own mind with accumulating and conflicting thoughts and constant questions, which all seem to be answered in the ninety minutes of game time on match days. I guess how complex or simple you perceive life to be comes down to the individual. The suffering, pain and sacrifices I endure for this game cannot even remotely compare to the satisfaction I derive from it. Just like an artist or an architect, I feel you can concoct your very own masterpiece when you have the ball at your feet. The pitch is the drawing board upon which you are creating, controlling and communicating in a sporting language understood throughout the whole globe. It makes a lot of sense when you hear how deftly the best players in the world are able to read the game no matter what their background.

It really is wonderful how this game can transport you to all four corners of the globe, where varying cultures, languages and upbringings all merge in this simple game of football. I have already had the privilege of playing in many parts of the world, and last year augmented this by moving to Portugal, where I am currently contracted to Benfica – the 'Red Devils' of Lisbon. It has been an amazing experience and an achievement of which I am extremely proud, seeing as only a matter of four seasons ago I was playing for my school team which was coached by George Huitker himself.

Mr H was a coach unlike any I have had to this day. He holds such a unique passion for this game and through my experience with the team during that season, he showed me how it's not always just about the footy.

He would agree that dancing with the ball is what matters the most.

Kaz Patafta

Pre-Match Entertainment: Not Just an Intro

I never thought I believed in sporting fairytales.

I don't see how anyone who has been involved in sport, at both the junior and professional levels, could possibly get romantic about it.

It would seem, more and more each day, the value of sport lies in unmitigated success. That is, success in terms of numbers: the number of wins strung together and, if you play at the professional level, the number of dollars you need in order to string together a sequence of unmitigated wins. And to keep doing so.

You would have thought, at least with our kids, that the simple fact that they are outdoors, getting fresh air and participating socially with others at their chosen game would be everything. Yet it seems inevitable that organised sport at any level desires to push things to the next plateau, where only success, defined in terms of solely winning, can give it any meaning.

It is then, particularly as a coach, that you start to see the world through dark, competitive, paranoid lenses...

There is always that flashy team of slick sporting spawn of Satan ready to knock you off your perch just when you're within a millimetre of grasping success, generally after years and years of poor luck, pure sweat and hard work. It doesn't help that these hellfire oppositions that execute you – and their skills – with a ruthless, clinical precision are rarely coached by some ex-World Cup winning pro, but more often than not by some unhealthily passionate, short-sighted, officious, pugnacious and balding family man with no life outside of the given sport and with nothing else to do on his weekends but drive his charges relentlessly toward successes he probably never had as a player, parent or person.

Yeah I know that's harsh. I'd better steady on. I'll take those glasses off.

I guess I can write nasty passages such as these because I myself have been sucked into that success-orientated vortex on many occasions. I too have been touched on the arm by that little devil, the one that sits smugly there on your left shoulder most Saturdays whispering sweet-nothings into your ear like *Win at all costs!* or *This referee is crap – abuse the hell outa him!* or *Get that useless kid off the paddock – he's not working hard enough and plays like a klutz!*

And then there are the 'Pohwni' (that is, Parents Of Hell With No Idea) to contend with. These are a bizarre and parochial tribe often seen sharpening their spears on match days. This lovable herd of dim-witted adults of all shapes and sizes, who have never played a single game of the sport in question, often congregate just metres outside of the coach's highly mystical aura. Pohwnis stand within earshot of the coach, close enough to hear all that he or she is saying to his charges because a) the coach may be quite wrong in his advice or instruction, b) the coach might miss something glaringly obvious somehow overlooked in being 'too close to the action' and c) they may eventually need ammunition with which to get the coach fired.

Pohwnis like to mingle perilously close to the playing field in order to be able to prod physically and mentally the players of both sides. This is of course very necessary when your goal in life is to encourage young sportspeople to reach their potential at any price, as kids these days – as we all know – can rarely do anything of their own volition and need to constantly be reminded of this.

Pohwnis also want coaches to push their kids *to the max*. They request things like *I want you to give him hell, coach!* or *She needs you to push her harder.* Yet when the unsuspecting or inexperienced coach follows any of these pohwni orders, he or she will be accused of bullying, be up before the club's equity tribunal and subsequently sent to coach the Siberian Under 7s for

21

thirty tortuous years unless a formal apology is made before the next game.

Lastly, Pohwnis can be as meek as Mother Teresa. But then do not be surprised should they quite suddenly sprout horns and pitchforks and direct a great deal of sporting and non-sporting abuse and frustration at the hapless individuals who have the misfortune of performing poorly as players on the sports field or – even worse – perform crappily as referees.

(Incidentally, these parents are also regularly seen as spectators at professional sporting fixtures, inevitably berating referees and, more importantly, their favourite overpaid players into performing at the optimum level. Of course, nothing short of total success will do if you're *getting paid* to play.)

I often wonder where this interminable demon of sporting supremacy and its associated, insatiable lust for success stems from. Is it because our own individual lives are so full of loss and disappointment that perhaps it could all be negated with a good ol'-fashioned win on the sports field? Or because the bigger, imperfect world is so lacking in miracles that we need, every so often, a sporting fairy tale to unravel before us, to keep us believing that they really do occur.

My father, for example, was a sporting man far removed

from any of these demons and existential questions. As you'll come to see, as an ardent supporter of teams such as the Dutch national football side, the Western Suburbs Magpies and any of his son's junior tennis, cricket or soccer outfits, he must have got relatively acclimatised to the idea that true sporting success was an elusive if not totally alien concept. Had he been alive as I write today, he would not be surprised to hear that the Dutch bowed out of Euro 2000 – on penalties once more – and that the Maggies have flown into the great, misty cloud of amalgamation in the sky.

But let's face it, we've had some reason to expect and be a little used to sporting success in this country. Bill Bryson succinctly put it in his recent book *Down Under*: '... Australia generally beats most people at most things.' As I write, Australia has uncannily won every professional sporting event from tiddlywinks to tennis. 1999 saw our nation place one international trophy beside another on its cluttered mantelpiece of triumphs. There's the women's netball World Cup to go nicely with the pair the men's cricket and rugby union teams collected, and then the addition of the Davis Cup for tennis, all of which proved that when it comes to sport we are a mighty world power. Hell, if we ever made the soccer – sorry, I mean *football* – World Cup finals, we'd probably win them too.

No, I'm getting a bit carried away now. That would be a sporting fairy tale.

As I've implied, success, like fairy tales, can inherently contain the dark side of the force. If I tell my four-year-old godson a winning bedtime fairy story, he's gonna want another just as dazzling and colourful – and never go to sleep. Like a good Pringle, once you've acquired one little taste of joy, you're going to desire the whole canister – and end up porky. Sadly, sometimes, success with a seductive capital $ helps folk forget what is significant, magical and lasting in sport and what it can truly offer a country, a state, a team or an individual. Like Christmas, its real meaning has little to do with making or spending money.

Les Murray, the SBS sports commentator, somewhat astutely commented in *A Century of Soccer: 100 Years of the World Game*:

> We should look forward to the next century with care and trepidation. The core element of football is its romance. And romance has not always been the core element of business.

And I couldn't agree more. Romance, fairy tales – these things should exist at the *heart* of all sport. Yet, as we commence the new century, other dubious things appear to have moved in and replaced them. A character in Thea Astley's novel *Drylands* moans that

> ...this country is round the bend over jumping and kicking and running and swimming and smashing into people all in the name of winning. It isn't about

sport any more. It's about power. And money. And politics. And it's boring. My God, it's boring.

When the desperate and greedy scramble for glory and power (in the Pohwni's case) and glory, power and cash become sporting directives (in the businessperson's), then sport will always be the big loser. 'Business' over 'romance' at the core of sport? Les Murray and Thea Astley are very shrewd in warning us of this trend.

Don't get me wrong. I understand I am hopelessly naive when it comes to sport and money. I am grateful I can turn on the television and have a reasonable variety of sport accessible to me most of the time, albeit littered at the end of every set, over or goal with a plethora of obnoxious ads. Yet the more dollar signs one sees in front of winners' cheques, on the suits in corporate boxes, on the admission price of tickets or in the cost of getting pay TV in order to see what was once free, the more I feel we're missing the point.

You have to pay a lot of money these days for a bit of sporting romance and a slice of fairy tale action.

I quite simply am too simple-minded to understand, for example, how paying Christian Vierri ninety billion lire will subsequently mean that he will do something significant, magical or lasting on the sports field for himself, his team or anybody else. The Pope certainly felt it was going a bit overboard. That money could, after all, be used to fill a lot of hungry mouths and fight disease in flood-stricken Mozambique.

When Christian left these Australian shores and 'made it' as a player in Spain and then the Italian Serie A, he might have inspired more kids with *this* fact: that it was possible to make it on the international soccer scene from Prairiewood High Under 15s. That's romance. That's a fairy tale. Accepting that ridiculously obese pay cheque is just business; putting a monetary value on his accomplishments ironically devalues them. (Incidentally, one Steve Waugh was also in that school's illustrious Bill Turner team, which was coached by Robbie Slater's elder brother, Peter.)

A final-second on-the-buzzer net by a cool Sharrelle McMahon, a fabulous Stephen Larkham field goal from near the halfway line, or an uncanny reversal of form by the seemingly down-and-out Woodies in that crucial Davis Cup rubber – all of which we were privileged to witness live to air – these impressive sporting moments etch themselves indelibly on the psyches of so many kids potting netballs, snapping field goals and whacking tennis balls in backyards, suburban ovals and school walls nationwide.

In my perfect world, Sharrelle, Stephen and the Woodies would have 'been there and done that' for no money, for the love of the game and the transcendent knowledge that they've done something significant, lasting and magical. And, in doing so, inspired a generation of Australian kiddies. I'd like to think that the money they received in having brand names sewn on their sweatbands, shirts, shorts and undies, or behind them on placards and boundaries, is purely irrelevant.

As an impressionable kiddie, I remember seeing a *Match of the Day* repeat of the funny-faced English 'keeper Gordon Banks blocking out Pele's bullet header in the 1970 World Cup preliminary round. It is a sporting moment that has stayed with me all my life, even though Gordon is a Pom. It led me, as a funny-faced aspiring goalkeeper, to realise that no shot on goal – no matter how perfectly timed or precisely struck – needs to be written off as unsaveable. I guess the same could be said about those seemingly unsaveable situations that life inevitably hurls at you, couldn't it? Thanks, Mr Banks. You perhaps started my romance with sport.

Then, in 1989, as a slightly older student of the university of life, I saw the Canberra Raiders make up a seemingly irretrievable deficit to steal the Grand Final (if memory serves me correctly, it was the *Winfield* Cup in those days) from a Balmain Tigers side that might have prematurely popped the champagne corks at half-time. I even went to the airport with my friends to greet the returning players – something I wouldn't do for Elle McPherson.

I've gone a bit too far again.

This was *Canberra*. This was *my home town*. There were some *home-grown* players in that garish lime-green line-up, some of whom had gone to *local* schools and had *real* jobs. One of those Grand Final try scorers regularly fixed the security systems at our school. (According to Laurie Daley, 'Chicka' Ferguson was such an undaunted, relaxed figure that his teammates would 'often find him asleep in the dressing room before a game'.) These were *real* people. My *birthplace* was on the map. Was it possible to be a winner and come from dull, soulless, diplomatic Canberra? Even in my discontented, maladjusted, bohemian post-school state, I was inspired. Surely that must have been a miracle?

Years later, well after I started as an English/Drama teacher and 'co-curricular' (I love that word) soccer coach at Radford College, Canberra, the Wallaby halfback George Gregan came to do his student-teaching prac at the school. It was 1994 and only months after he made The Tackle in the Tri-Nations tournament, sending All Black Jeff Wilson hurling into touch and Gregan himself well and truly into the international sporting spotlight. (Gregan was rushed into the Radford staff side for the annual staff vs student touch football fixture. His passes were so flat and fast that, if caught, they would send the receiver hurling into touch as well. Despite that, the staff mysteriously won the staff–

student fixture, which made for a pleasant change that year.) That George Gregan was doing ordinary things like studying, worrying about a future beyond sport and playing touch with the aged at lunchtime, well, it all sent a necessary if unsettling shiver around the playgrounds and prep rooms of the school. Then the over-achieving smart alec went and won a World Cup to boot. I'm sure Radford would be more than happy in having you in their PE Department when your rugby days are over, George.

Yet with sport it is sometimes hard to see the wood for the trees. In many ways, sport can consume you, like the desire to eat everything on the McDonalds menu the second before you order, despite the knowledge deep down that this may not be the best thing to do before a footy training or a home-cooked dinner.

There are things in life other than sport that maybe *should* consume your time, a fact very hard for a lot of us die-hard sport junkies to swallow. There are fields like science, art and philanthropy (which I always thought was about collecting stamps), and other things like spirituality and relationships, to name a few, that are possibly just as – if not more – important than the desire to throw, kick and whack an object around a cow paddock.

Or so I've been told.

There's probably a rotund major poet writing and wringing his heart out there somewhere, flailing his soul in some small country town just off the coast, about to write something so mind-bogglingly perceptive and profound that it could change the whole way in which we view the world and ourselves. But if I were to ask you if you knew Les Murray, you'd probably say he commentates for SBS soccer. One out of two.

In January 2000, I stepped onto a plane bound for the UK with a young soccer team I'd coached for around five years at the junior club level, since they started high school as timid Year 7s waiting to get their heads flushed down the dunny by the older students. Without trying to make too much of a statement of intent or jumping the gun, I've learned a great deal about myself, human beings and the nature of sport in the relatively short period of my association with these little creeps. Although at times it may have *seemed* that our sporting journey was far from miraculous, romantic or fairy tale, with the benefit of hindsight, it has been all of these things – despite errors made along the way.

The last decade of coaching junior soccer has certainly been a vital part of a learning continuum that began almost two and a half decades earlier, when my father first put a ball, like the world, at my feet. From that day, sport has never been far away.

And so, for the last year or two, that little demon of self-indulgence has constantly returned to nestle on my left shoulder, compelling me to sit at a word processor and tap out a pretentious, warts-and-all memoir of all that has occurred since those West Woden Juventus trials twenty-five years ago on the rolling green ovals of Holman Street, Curtin. *And what the hell,* whispered the horned little freak on my shoulder, *while you're at it, totally indulge. Why not throw some random opinions, travel tips, photography and poetry into the soup?*

Coaching a team sport has the potential to be one of the most singularly self-indulgent things a person can do in the guise of promoting the well-being, success, development and growth of others. Forgive me. But I'm sure it comes a close second to writing your memoirs.

This book is not written for 'business'. It is not written for success. It will make very little money. It is, partly, written for the ghost of my father, but definitely not to exorcise him. We need more friendly ghosts roaming this planet giving us other-worldly clues as to where the value of sport truly lies. To tell us it's all hidden somewhere in an unassuming place where the cash zombies and the win-hungry walk forever blind.

I once wrote in a poem about sport that 'this clumsy cliché of winning and losing is done for the self, no less'. I know the same could be said about this book.

Regardless, I hope that someone out there can find in these little stories about my father, my soccer team and a trip to the United Kingdom a little more of what is, to me, significant, magical and lasting in sport. And to learn from my phenomenal list of mistakes.

Even as I was stepping onto that Emirates flight to London, I was beginning to see the impending trip as the fairy tale-flavoured icing on a big sporting cake, the ingredients of which were supplied a long time ago by my Dad. And I am coming to realise how fatuous my opening statement is.

If sport can teach people that living fully and actively in the world is essentially a healthy thing for your body and soul – then that's great. If it can make you notice, appreciate and develop aspects of yourself and other people – then that's great too. If it helps you to focus on the more substantial, lasting rewards of life – that's magic. If it takes you places you've never been before – that's a bonus. And if it allows you to inspire and be inspired by impressive people – be they overpaid sport stars or penniless legends like my father – then that's bloody marvellous.

Then maybe I do believe in sporting fairy tales.

Easter Raid

The crowd ascends
as the Raiders run on.
A father thumps his son:
Hurry, it's starting!

I think of my father,
who longed to see a stadium rise,
back when the Raiders were only promise
on Seiffert's small country backlot.

The crowd jeers
at the men from the East.
I shift, uneasy;
as a child they were
The Raiders to me:
immortal, victorious.

But that was a time long gone,
and the home side draws first blood.
Next to me mother applauds;
she adores this chanting of litany,
hailing of heroes,
homage of hands.

In the centre, the purge continues.
And for a winning moment:
my father is resurrected,
my mother happy;
I cheer like a child,
and allow myself
to forget
and lose myself in the moment.

The crowd will leave exulted,
souls elevated this Easter.
For today, of all days,
there will be a mighty victory
and a resurgence of the spirit,
perhaps hinting that I
wasn't the only one
temporarily
lifted.

1. The First Half: Not Just a Father

It is a wise father that knows his own child.
– William Shakespeare, *The Merchant of Venice*, circa late 16th century.

You go in goals and just shut up.
– John Huitker, circa 1975

One of the greatest gifts my Dad gave me in his lifetime was the quantity of sport he frequently exposed me to. It became the norm that, come the weekend, Saturday morning was reserved for actually *playing* sport and the time that followed was exclusively and lovingly reserved for viewing it.

Every weekend we would be off to see either the Canberra Arrows, the Canberra Raiders, the Canberra Cannons or some local tennis star take on some inter-state competition at their respective codes. And if these teams or individuals weren't at home, there was always our local West Woden Juventus Soccer team to cheer for or the lure of a lazy afternoon in front of the box watching the VFL. If I was really lucky, we'd even go interstate to catch some cricket, rugby or tennis. The code never mattered. In my formative years, I attempted nearly every sport except croquet.

Even when he was very sick with cancer and hospitalised, I remember vividly his sheer delight when the Australian cricket team won back a consolation Test against the then indestructible West Indies in Sydney, early in 1989. Dad always had a belief in Allan Border's underutilised bowling ability; father had a gift for spotting talent where it wasn't glaringly apparent. As it turned out, the Aussie captain turned the test, picking up eleven wickets for under a hundred runs in an inspirational spell of spin bowling. It was the best bowling display by an Australian captain in the history of the sport. When things are dire, Border might have said, you can sometimes find something within yourself to save a situation.

For once, the underdogs won. And damn the cliché: sport was the winner. And that was everything that mattered.

Albeit for a short period of time.

Mal Meninga, on the other hand, was a captain who perplexed my father and me. Don't get us wrong, we thought it was very good-natured of Mal to come from sunny Queensland to play rugby league for cold, classless Canberra. It was just that, whenever Mal lined up to take a shot at goal, we'd all have to turn away to Mecca, hold hands and energetically pray. His radar was unpredictably wonky.

Despite the fact that the lush lime-green Raiders had actually been seen in a Grand Final back in 1986 (they lost to Manly 18–8), we never really felt we'd see the day when the Winfield Cup would come home to roost in the nation's capital. Even in 1990, as Mum and I watched the Green Machine clinically destroy my childhood heroes, Eastern Suburbs, 66–4 in the biggest defeat in Roosters' history, with Meninga contributing five tries and nine goals, we never dared dream they could go all the way *again*.

Never let anyone, Meninga might have said, *ever tell you that you are past your use-by date.* In 1989, a little under a year since Dad had died, the Raiders won the premier-ship. The so-called has-been banana-bender with the wayward radar took us to three more Grand Finals, winning two of them, then gracefully retiring after scoring the final try in the third.

Even though I had nothing personally or directly to do with the Raiders' successes and have, in truth, never played a game of rugby league in my life, I believe it was the first time I had ever felt that I had been a part of something significant. A sporting fairy tale had actually unfolded here in Canberra and, oh, how I desperately hoped some of it would rub off on a team I coached.

But that's a story for a little later.

Sport would rarely be associated with fairy tales for my dear father.

Being a Dutchman, he was quite used to seeing his national side blow soccer World Cups and European competitions. After seeing the Netherlands get pipped at the post in World Cup Finals in 1974 and 1978, he was allowed some joy in the last year of his life, when the Dutch national side led by Ruud Gullit won the 1988 European Cup 2–0 against Russia.

What's more, in goal there existed a geeky-looking beanpole named Hans van Breukelen. (Geeky features, I'm afraid, are synonymous with goalkeepers. I cite van Breukelen, Schmeichel, Bosnich, Banks and myself as examples.) Hans was not only exceptionally good at keeping balls from hitting the net behind him, but also stopped a crucial Russian penalty in the '88 final. I always glow on the inside when 'keepers stop penalties.

This Dutch team was definitely a glowing exception to the rule that any team Dad supported would never see success. And he deserved to see more.

Regardless, it is a relief to know that in life they will exist, these little exceptions. Except maybe in Chicago. I recently read with interest in Bill Bryson's *Notes from a Big Country* about the hapless Chicago Cubs, a team which has not made the World Series since 1938. Writes Bryson,

> Whatever it takes – losing seventeen games in a row, letting easy balls go through their legs, crashing comically into each other in the outfield – you can be certain the Cubs will manage it. They have been doing this, reliably and efficiently, for over half a century... It's not easy being a baseball fan because baseball fans are a hopelessly sentimental bunch and there is no room for sentiment in something as widely lucrative as an American sport.

I cannot help but feel that, if Dad had been interested in American baseball, the closet sentimentalist that he was, he would have empathised strongly and sworn firm allegiance to the unfulfilled Chicago Cubs.

Dad always had a quiet, world-weary acceptance of all the hardships life occasionally threw before him. While I constantly raged against the world, Dad gently sailed on through it. It was just as well he had this serene temperament. As a committed spectator and occasional coach of some of his son's aspiring junior West Woden Juventus and Marist College soccer teams across a decade between 1975 and 1985, he had to accept quietly a hell of a lot of losses. (Towards the end of his life, in accepting his terminal sickness, he became the most gracious, modest, unassuming human being I have ever known.)

He must have rolled his eyes when he first saw me play, trying out for West Woden Juventus Under 8s on a small, suburban oval in Holman Street, Curtin. I now frequently jog past Holman Street and feel a pang of sadness at how it has been abandoned. Weed has become the only plant life visible or tough enough to live through its cracked, dry and neglected surface. Tell me, is there anything harder to swallow than to see a place so significant to your childhood either left to rot or have a condominium or car park built on it?

Yet it was on that surface, which back then was a tad more lush and green, where I first tripped over my laces chasing a soccer ball and landed with a dull *thwack!* on the turf. Do you understand now why my Dad was a closet sentimentalist?

My father had been a soccer player himself, and seeing his son trip over his feet must have, at the very least, made his spirits plummet to somewhere near his own. I can remember saying after one half-hour trial of soccer that I wanted to quit and try another sport like finger knitting. But all the gear had been bought – my nifty shin pads and leather boots – and I was to give it another attempt. If I knew what was good for me. *Try your best. Then decide.*

My childhood hero was a Russell Fairfax from Eastern Suburbs Rugby League club. It's OK. I am aware he is not a soccer player. This rugby union convert from Randwick had long blond locks, which seemed to freeze horizontally with the speed in which he bolted from the fullback position and he was, to me at least, the coolest sportsman on the planet.

When the Roosters won back-to-back Grand Finals in 1974/75, I decided to grow my hair, bleach it and convert to rugby league, something which in my household was as abhorrent as voting Labor. Although I thought I emulated Fairfax quite well when scoring tries during the Holy Trinity Primary School lunch-hour grudge matches against the girls' kindergarten team, it was probably for the best I never took up rugby league. I probably would have fallen over *before* the opposition tackled me. I was never allowed to have long, flowing locks either.

As it transpired, I made the Under 8 Division 3 soccer side – and there were none lower. I felt that Division 30 would've been more appropriate after that first trial. I was pretty hopeless but lived comforted in the knowledge that there was one in the team who was a bigger klutz than I – the goalkeeper, Zelco. While I kept kicking fresh-air shots when playing at left midfield (the position on any team where a coach puts a player he wishes to hide), attacking opposition forwards would ping them at Zelco, who couldn't catch a cold in Iceland.

Our coach, Pat Norris, was obviously a genius, because he worked out a way of improving a seemingly helpless situation. He switched Zelco and me around. He informed my father after an early round match that he was going to try me out in goal. This would have possibly relieved and simultaneously stressed Dad. I couldn't possibly play any worse in this new position, he must have figured, and I would be emulating him – Dad had himself been a goalkeeper. But then it was *just* possible, wasn't it, that I would make a goose of myself there too.

Dad was born Jan George Huitker in Cirebon, in the Dutch East Indies, on 13 August 1922. (When he emigrated to Australia, he changed his name to John, obviously not wishing to be confused with the middle Brady Bunch sister.) He was sent to Holland for his high school education where, as a young swinger, he had kept goals and flipped meat patties at the quaintly named Gemeentelijke Hogere Burger School. After leaving GHBS, he studied horticulture and botany in Boskoop, while he also 'kept in the lower divisions for clubs in Utrecht between 1937 and 1941. That was before the global nuisance of World War II disrupted and seemed to wrap up his playing days. He must have been a reasonably swift and athletic 'keeper. My Uncle Theo told me he once broke his collarbone on a goalpost diving for a penalty. This is a hard thing to do. I didn't have the heart to ask my uncle if he saved it.

Due to the war and the slow process of emigration, courtship and the subsequent immigration of the future Mrs Huitker that followed in December 1963, my parents married comparatively late in life two years later and I was indeed lucky to be born at all. Mum, being well into her forties, may have left things a tad late, a trait which has stayed with her well into her seventies. I was obviously blessed in having athletic parents, as I imagine producing babies at their age would require a stamina not normally associated with people of that age group. As an old schoolmate said to me, my parents scored that golden goal in extra time.

The year was 1967. The Beatles, all sporting long, flowing locks of hair and silly moustaches were simply getting better all the time and putting the finishing touches on the wonderfully psychedelic classic *Sgt Pepper's Lonely Hearts Club Band* while my adopted English Football Club, Coventry City, doing the best they could as well, had finally entered the elite ranks of the First Division competition. I didn't know it at the time, but this band and this team would follow me around for many years to come.

Mum told me that when I was born I looked like a rabbit. That may explain why I was born so close to Easter. Regardless, our family doctor was quite concerned over the real possibility that there would be complications due to Mum's age and the fact that I was six weeks premature. (These days, I'd be lucky to make it to things six *minutes* early.) He proclaimed that Mum, at forty-three, and after three days of pushing hard, had produced a miracle birth. I tend to agree.

You had a hard head, Mum told me. *And you were hard work.*

If only she knew what was to follow.

Thus it came about, in 1975, that things had reached full circle and I was to become the Under 8 Division 3 version of Jan – sorry, *John* – Huitker. Naturally, I protested to him and he sensitively and tersely said to me those famous words, *You go in goals and just shut up.*

I can remember spending nearly every afternoon that week at Holman Street, getting extra tuition from Dad. He taught me how to catch, collect, fist and deflect shots; jump, leap and dive after balls; take goal kicks; and throw my body fearlessly at approaching attackers. He persisted with me, one on one, at every opportunity. I would have to save what seemed like a hundred penalties and, if I didn't stop them, would have to chase the bloody ball for miles behind the posts, sometimes into the creek that ran adjacent to the fields. I'd then bring the dripping, algae-coated ball back, get between the goalposts and start again. Yep, repetition is at the heart of improvement. As a Canadian theatre director, Walter Learning, would constantly say to me as an aspiring actor on an entirely different playing field nearly twenty years later, *'Répétition' is the French word for 'rehearsal'*. And after the '98 World Cup and Euro 2000, who could argue with the French?

When I look back on things, it was those afternoons with Dad which flood back vividly into the memory, more so than any particular matches or small victories. That father with his boy, training feverishly as the sun dragged the last vestiges of light behind the Brindabellas. That was quality time.

As a coach, you learn that these quiet moments spent one on one with players, nurturing and encouraging at a more intense level, showing a personal interest beyond the team training sessions, *that's* when things can really happen. That's when players realise you do care for them as developing individuals as much as for the team in its entirety. And this is what good coaches can bequeath to their charges: a sense that the well-being of each and every player is intrinsically linked with the development and well-being of the team as a whole. It's what some coaches, too busy worrying about the well-being of their individual 'stars' or maintaining a team's unbeaten climb to the top of a dung heap, can sometimes miss.

As it turned out, I saved a penalty in my first game without damaging my collarbone. I had seen about a thousand leave Dad's clogs in fading light the week before, so I didn't understand what the fuss was all about. As we were one goal up, and it was in the dying minutes of the match, I was led to believe by everyone's reaction that what I had done in stopping the flimsy shot *was* relatively significant. I remember thinking the penalty taker didn't take penalties half as nonchalantly or trickily as Dad and it was much easier to actually see the ball in the middle of the day.

Anyway, from that moment, I never turned back. I had found my niche. It's funny how you just fall into things in life.

Thanks, Dad.

I began to watch with renewed and diligent interest the exploits of goalkeepers. I would sit behind West Woden Juventus's senior team's net and happily fetch stray shots or clearances for their Number 1, John Janeczko. And then, at half-time, Dad and I would swap sides with Janeczko and the team, and resume work, study and retrieval for another forty-five minutes. God knows what Janeczko must have thought as we reappeared week in, week out. But hey – we were fans – that's what they do!

Then one night, watching *Match of the Day*, Jimmy Hill decided to show some classic moments of sport and replayed The Gordon Banks Save. I had read about it. Dad had raved about it. And now, I was going to actually see it.

I wasn't disappointed. Banks's dive to his right, impossibly deflecting Pele's header up and over the bar, was to stay in the video machine inside my head forever. Even as I write, that tape is far from worn out. What a save! Go Banksie!

Over the rest of the season we won a few games, lost more, but appeared to never be disgraced by scorelines. Looking over old team newsletters (which my mother religiously saved), it would seem I had 'a good game' more often than not. Zelco was having the time of his life as a field player, occasionally giving away free kicks when he forgot that he wasn't a goalkeeper any more and subsequently tried to catch balls that were too hard to control with his feet or body. It was a happy season as we all grew accustomed to our on-field roles and Pat Norris, the genius that he was, steered the helm for my first happy year in sport. God love him, wherever he is now.

Dad, who would always stand and chat patiently and unobtrusively with me by the goalposts during games, gently transformed me from an awkward participant to a confident player. Whenever I made a good save, he would tell me so in his laconic, unsentimental Dutch-accented way: *Not bad.* And if I was collecting a ball from the back of the net, he'd take a drag from his cigarette and silently blow out our frustration so that, by the time the smoke disappeared, the blunder had long been forgotten.

In those days, teams in the bottom half of the draw were still involved on Finals Day. These luckless sides got to play off for what was called 'The Minor Cup'. A knockout system ensued, from which the 'best of the bottom' finally got to play in a pseudo-Grand Final situation. This actually did wonders for a lot of shaky self-esteems.

After a happy first season, we actually started to play some nice soccer and our centre forward, Sean, was starting to score with some consistency and flair. His dad was an ebullient snowy-haired Pom, so everyone figured Sean had it 'in the genes'. Sean was allowed to have long hair, so I was jealous of more than just his soccer skill.

We won the Minor Cup against Weston Creek. The

scoreline seems to be lost in my memory, but I do remember the team jelled as a cohesive unit and Sean no doubt scored the match winner, precocious smart arse that he was. We were given crummy little blue certificates from the Junior League which really pissed us all off. Hell hath no fury like an Under 8's scorn. Where were the trophies?

Let me digress a little here.

People who live outside of the sporting culture have no idea of the importance of a trophy to a sportsperson. And no, I am not being pathetic. Ask any sportsperson whether they've got a cabinet full of 'em or a desperately empty mantelpiece: trophies are *it*.

Sure, they are crappily sculptured, fragile ornamentals which, in those days, always had significant limbs breaking off them, but to a junior socceroo of eight, or a senior professional of twenty-eight, they are highly desired and subsequently treasured items. When the West Woden Juventus Senior team won the Ampol Cup that year – some of our Under 8 Division 3 Minor Cup success obviously inspiring them to go all the way – I remember seeing my hero, goalkeeper John Janeczko, cuddling his like a well-worn childhood teddy bear. And he was a grown-up. And my idol!

After never receiving one bloody trophy during my

entire junior career, I had become resigned to the fact that they actually were as elusive as a Dutch World Cup victory. And yes, the fact of never winning one consequently loitered in my psychological make-up well past adolescence, making me one of the more driven, pathetic, sideline psychos I was later to become as a junior coach.

Over the following year, I became blooded to the reality of junior sport politics. At that point, having never been coached by a father who had a son in the team, I was kept innocent of the talons of nepotism, a pimple on the face of all junior sport.

Sean and other nifty Division 3 players 'with some potential' were whisked away to the higher divisions and subsequently replaced by 'incorrectly placed' klutzes from Divisions 1 and 2 the year before. I could not understand why the fact that I admired Sean as a player and a person was not a governing factor in his remaining in Division 3 with me. It was then and there I learned that friendship within sport would always be a tenuous thing. And that loyalty meant little. Sean went up and I stayed where I was.

I rolled my eyes, seasoned veteran of one year that I was, when players with as much in the way of ball skills as I had a year earlier found their way into the team in front of me. There were at least half a dozen players in my line of sight tripping helplessly over their laces and falling face first into the turf. We even had a girl in our team, a tough bitch called Penny, who played in the back line and won my instant respect (that is, I forgot she was a girl after a while). Zelco had evidently quit the game, possibly to try his 'hand' at something more appropriate, like basketball.

Over the season, I was very busy in my Division 3 goals. The newsletters indicate (thanks again, Mum!) that we had a tough time of it, and I was stretched in goal to keep the opposition tallies down. But the good thing about being in a weak side is that you can never be complacent about anything except the certainty of defeat and you'll always get a good hit-out if you're the 'keeper. My skills developed nicely throughout that second year.

My school, Marist College, had started to make inroads as a 'club' side, and offered my father (who up until then had been content to be my personal trainer) a position as coach of their fledgling Under 10 Division 1 side. I had developed an arrogance goalkeeping behind the worst team on the planet and figured I could cope with the huge leap, up two divisions, to the big time. I figured I couldn't be any busier than I had been.

So, in keeping with the spirit of the times, I trendily left friendship and loyalty by the wayside and switched to my school side. In doing so, I managed to convince some schoolmates who had played at West Woden – a Hungarian/Turkish sharpshooter named Alfred, a rough okker defender named Chris (who was infamous off the field for chasing people with axes when perplexed), and an unassuming, hard-working midfielder named Peter – to defect to my father's glamorous new team. My only regret was that Sean didn't go to Marist. Now he *would* have been worth ninety billion lire.

Over the next two years, possibly the happiest of my life, I got to see a lot of my schoolmates and my father, who was now my soccer coach, quite regularly. In retrospect, I can only marvel at his achievement. We were relatively unskilled by Division 1's lofty standards, but we were a gutsy, gritty and passionate little outfit – something I like to think is characteristic of Huitker-coached teams.

Alfred could still find the back of the net with ease, especially off corners, which became a bit of a trademark of his. Chris would continue to (metaphorically) axe down any opposition players who had the audacity to attempt to pass him. Peter continued to plug away doggedly in the guts. And we managed to pick up a diminutive little terrier – an army brat by the name of Michael who would run under the legs of opposition players and suddenly appear in front of them like a magician's pigeon to steal possession, then flutter away.

That year, I had taken to wearing a Geelong Number 23 jumper. Many people would question why exactly I was wearing it. Did I know what sporting code I was playing? Dad would explain that I was a perennially confused little boy. But regardless, the fact that my new post-Fairfax sporting hero was a Geelong full forward named Larry Donohue didn't greatly concern him. Nor did the fact that the jumper looked horribly out of place with our navy blue team tops.

Donohue was a gem for the Cats, and made some particularly acrobatic marks at times, a quality I tried to emulate when corners and high shots came swirling into the goal area. Like Dad, I loved all sports and never understood why people had to get into heated spats about one being superior to the other.

Dad at training was a revelation to me. It is only now I realise that when he took this team on he was a sprightly fifty-five. My Aunty Willy, a family friend whom I confided to when I was four years old that I was in fact Superman, recently made the point over dinner that my father had an energy, drive and willingness to be involved in all the facets of his son's life that was *far stronger and more dedicated than any father of twenty-five.* I feel somewhat ashamed that I'm only realising this sort of thing now, when it's all too late to say *Thanks* to his face in the living years, to steal that song's phrase.

Possibly because of his age, Dad was not a coach who moved around a lot; instead, he commanded respect with stillness and silence, much as he did socially. He used to smoke Kool cigarettes, which I guess was in keeping with his personality, and suck on crystal-flavoured Lifesavers. He was one of that sort of volcanic coaches. When he finally blew his top, which was inevitably due to my taking far too many liberties as the coach's son, hell would freeze over and all of us would, in turn, freeze to the spot and listen very very intently to whatever followed. We would never push it any further. Enough was enough. *Genoeg* is *genoeg*.

And then he'd continue on his merry way as if nothing had happened, almost as if his explosion was an act – a disarming trait my players say I have inherited. Whatever the case, we both innately felt that anger has extreme limitations as a motivator or a disciplinary force.

My 'punishment' for being a supreme attention-seeking moron at training would always be the same: Dad would not talk to me about my behaviour at all on the return trip home. In the quiet car, after the episode in question, he'd just chew on his crystal-flavoured

Lifesavers and I would always inevitably feel as if I had been punished. To this day I have no idea how my Dad disciplined without ever directly addressing any issues or nurturing any guilt. With his body language and loud silences, he somehow allowed you to fix yourself up. Plain and simple.

So it followed that at trainings he allowed a team to fix itself up as well. It takes a special sort of coach to pull this off, especially with ten-year-olds. At times, things would seem random, chaotic and seemingly unstructured. But he was never afraid to let kids have fun at training, something that can be missed in the more competitive coach's manuals.

Although all of his drills were games-based and enjoyably, if not frivolously, competitive (you'd usually win a packet of lollies, which he'd make the winning team distribute with the losing one), he would never be afraid to stop things, bring us in and discuss any specifics that needed work. Without giving any indication which team members were the culprits he'd say, *We gave away a lot of ball...with foul throws. And we're doing it now again – here at training. Bah!*

He'd take a drag of his Kool cigarette, shaking his head in a 'how-could-we-be-such-cretins' sort of bemused Dutch admonishment. He'd ask us what the correct technique for throwing the ball actually was, working from our knowledge before appending his own. He'd subtly and humorously demonstrate the right method, using one of us as a guinea pig (and sometimes pipsqueak Michael as the ball). Next, before we knew it, we'd be having a lolly-driven competition to see who could throw the furthest, the most accurately, the most comfortably for our teammates to trap, and, most importantly, who had improved most of all. By the time we'd resumed our scratch match, throw-ins were a fun and rectified part of our team game.

To be truthful, by the weekend game this was all well and truly forgotten. C'mon. We were Under 10s. *Remember training!* we'd hear this world-weary Dutch-accent holler from the lines, followed by some theatric, rhetorical mutterings for the parents and pohwnis.

At matches, especially when things were going awry, he would always keep yelling out instructions and encouragement, undeterred by savage scorelines. He kept pohwnis at bay by simply turning his back on them and walking elsewhere. He understood that they'd be rendered impotent without an audience. His attitude was similar with abrasive opposition coaches, except he'd walk further away.

I guess with age comes collected wisdom and, with Jan – sorry, *John* – Huitker, it was a gentle wisdom, pearls of which would be imparted so quietly and off-handedly that they wouldn't migrate from the ear to the brain until a small period of time had elapsed. He was an amateur coach with professional calm; more than we deserved. I realise now just how hard he consistently worked. After coaching my own junior teams, I respect even more his saintly patience, persistence and presence across a long junior season. It could not have come easily.

When I am his age, I have every intention of being a cantankerous, selfish, stamp-collecting ol' coot who enjoys sitting at home listening to Mantovani and complaining about the state of the nation. But this man, at fifty-five, was doing the hard yards in the lion's den. He was sharing our little frustrations and smaller joys and, despite the toll it must have taken on those tired old bones, he unfailingly reappeared every training, undaunted by results, our unpredictable behaviour or a bad day at the office. An heroic constant. He was a gritty, real human being.

I won my second Minor Cup that year under Dad, no mean feat for a team green to the Division 1 competition. But of course, after winning something relatively significant for only the second time in my life, the Junior League once more saw fit to reward my team with a blue cardboard certificate which was presented to us at school months later. Is there anything more demeaning than achieving something you perceive to be grand...

and then getting a certificate for it? I thought not. And fumed for the remainder of 1977.

Dad must have known that my desire for receiving a trophy had now reached psychologically disturbing proportions. He went out and had a trophy made for me as Best Team Player. It was the first I'd ever received and is one I still proudly have today. One of the arms fell off and for years was crudely held in place by sticky tape. I tried to super-glue it back on years later but the persistent appendage fell off again, this time disappearing into the vortex of a vacuum cleaner. I look at that one-armed trophy periodically. You know, in those moments when you feel pathetically sentimental, it fills a hole.

I recently laser-copied a photo of that Under 10 side and framed it in an artificial-gold frame, where it sits on its stand, behind the amputated plaster figurine that preceded it. We had just won the Minor Cup – Alfred, Chris, Michael and I (in my trusty Geelong jumper) have faces and stoops that suggest man had yet to evolve from the ape – and Dad, with that serious, coachy look he reserved for team photographs, has his hand gently resting on Peter's shoulder, looking straight at the camera with his determined yet unflappable face.

Inside, you knew he was very proud at turning this motley crew into something more than they would have been had he not been around.

It was 1978. Michael left Canberra. His dad probably had to recruit and kill people somewhere else. We went to Europe for a family holiday. And watched, in my aunty's little Utrecht apartment, Argentina totally depress the Dutch nation for the second time in two World Cup finals, with a 3–1 defeat in extra time. I remember wanting to spend the next day, sympathetic eleven-year-old that I was, hugging every despondent Hollander that I met. It's a wonder my arms didn't fall off. Both Dad and I knew it was all our fault. In selfishly winning our second Minor Cup the year before, we essentially *robbed* Holland of all its fairy tale stuff, dooming them to a second season in hell. That's how it works.

It's funny with sportspeople – how they actually believe such crap. That what they do or wear or how they act actually has a profound effect on a game being played even on the other side of the planet. I know someone who used to believe that stepping on a crack in the footpath gave opposition sides a goal on the weekend. I also know someone who believes his junior side won't win on weekends unless he's wearing his trusty FC Utrecht supporter's cap. And has had a morning jog.

With Marist not wishing to put a side into Division 1 the following year, I returned to West Woden for Under

12s, along with Alfred, Chris and Peter, where I was pleasantly reunited with goal thief Sean, this time at the top flight. We all made a pact to balance things in the cosmos by beating any sides that had Argentines among their ranks. Sadly, there was not a single Argentine boy playing in Under 12s that year. So we had to imagine that Croatia Deakin was in fact *Argentina* Deakin in order to get any satisfaction. And they thumped us anyway.

I played out my junior years there at West Woden Juventus, mostly in first division teams, before being distracted by my senior studies and the lure of things literary, musical, thespian and feminine - not necessarily in that order.

It wasn't quite the same, not having Dad at the helm in these later teams. Like me in my later coaching years, he probably had to decide whether his own skill level as a player would act as an impediment to the development of his players' more rapidly improving skills. Nonetheless, he remained omnipresent on match days, leaning on my goalpost (which is banned these days) and frequently took over as assistant coach when needed.

We continued to see lots of sport, hoping that an elusive sporting fairy tale would still one day unfold before our very eyes. The Canberra Cannons gave us a ray of hope throughout the 80s, when they won three NBL titles. But as basketball was a sport as bizarre and incomprehensible to Dad and me as dwarf throwing, it didn't feel as if we owned or were a legitimate part of those championships. So we had to persist with the Raiders, the Arrows and Wally Masur (whose father I once played doubles with at Yarralumla Tennis Club).

We were keen supporters of Canberra City Soccer Club (who became the terrifyingly titled Canberra Arrows in 1981). But like the current Canberra Cosmos, the Arrows seldom fired to light up our dark, starless night skies. Nevertheless, I was still thrilled to see, week in and week out, local heroes such as Tony Brennan, Steven Hogg and the acrobatic 'keeper Steve Hoszowski (who became my brand new, post-Janeczko idol). I was to eventually see each of these fellows very close-up, on the sidelines as coaches of rival junior oppositions. Harry Williams, an Arrow and ex-Australian World Cup squad member of 1974, even fronted up in an opposition side for an indoor soccer match against a team I player-managed. Coaching and playing against your childhood heroes can be quite disarming, yet also thrilling in quite a pathetic way, especially if you're successful against them. I rarely was.

Perhaps the next most influential of coaches I had as an impressionable teenager was a rugged, stocky little Italian man named Frank Brunacci. In my wild teenage imagination, I was certain he was a seasoned vet from some *real* Juventus side who had watched with dismay the Australian squad's somewhat ordinary performance at the 1974 World Cup, then decided to come to the sunburnt country in order to educate the convicts how better to manoeuvre their ball'n'chains around cowpats on the soccer paddock.

Frank was a hard man. He showed no emotion at training or on the sidelines at games. I really admire this in a person but, being volatile by nature, I cannot comprehend it in any meaningful way. There was no question about Brunacci's passion for the sport, but if sport's function was to 'let off a bit of steam', I'd imagine he could internally and single-handedly power the entire Snowy Mountains Scheme. My erratic, hormonal, inconsistent and underachieving West Woden side was no less frustrating now than it was for poor ol' Pat Norris all those years ago.

Once, injured after throwing myself at the feet of a reckless attacker, I rolled on the ground in agony expecting praise for the courageous save and sympathy for my considerable pain. I heard Brunacci, looking down at me with his Joe Pesci face softly say, *Geet up or geet orff.* Dad, leaning against the goalpost behind me, chuckled. These two men are responsible for lifting my pain threshold to places abnormal for a teenage boy. What doesn't kill you makes you stronger, right?

At this stage of my blossoming career, I had taken to

doing spectacular dives and would, with very few exceptions, deflect the ball away rather than catch it. George Banks is somewhat to blame here. He made it look so classy when you parried away saves. So I tried to make every save look like his blinder against Pele.

It also didn't help that, when I was in Under 8s, I noticed the sideline parents would get really excited when I 'dove'n'deflected' – heaps more than when I just caught the melon. But Brunacci, unfazed by applause or acrobatics simply said, *Catch eet more, show-orff. You not need to jump jump jump en tap tap tap eet away so much. Stoop eed.*

But Frank was always a direct contrast to Dad. Wise coaches always know the best time to say those important things to players. In fact, Dad didn't say anything for weeks about my predilection for deflecting until, casually during a game we were winning, he leant around the post and said, *Try to hang onto it. Whenever you can.* I assumed he was talking about footballs.

This was towards the end of my playing days, when my concentration became wayward and that adolescent hesitancy started to creep into my game – that realisation that I possibly wasn't going to be the next John Janeczko, Steve Hoszowki or Hans van Breukelen. It was then that I needed more than ever a mentor like my Dad.

Angry with the ugly, unfair and uninterested world, I decided that, since I had never been in a team that had won anything significant, what was the point in playing week in and week out? Self-pity oozed from every pore. I started to deflect balls on purpose, costing my side a goal or two, but allowing me to have my cranky little adolescent rebellion in front of an unappreciative audience.

My teammates would say, *Hold on to it, you tosser.* I heard a local Pohwni say, *I don't think George has got it any more.* I heard Frank say, *Weelyum can go een goalz – if you arr seek orff eet.* These were not the best responses to make to my questioning antics. What was the point of continuing with something when you were never significantly achieving anything? Why was that so hard for all of you to comprehend?

It's up to you, said laconic Jan – sorry, *John* – Huitker one Saturday afternoon, leaning on the goalpost, exhaling smoke. And, in typical John Huitker fashion, he'd leave you at the controls of your own hazy destiny, but always knowing that he was somewhere nearby should the plane really plummet.

Was it up to me to stop deflecting catchable shots? Was it up to me to realise the fact that, lousy as losing was, winning wasn't everything? Was it up to *me* to decide whether I was enjoying soccer? And whether to persist with it or not? Was it I who had to fix these problems?

I realise now how hard that must have been for him to say... *It's up to you.* It was brave to leave all those questions for me to answer, some of which have taken up until now. I've a slow mind. He knew me well enough to know where I was heading with my ponderous thought processes, as wise coaches are wont to do. And fathers.

And I knew him well enough to know that somewhere deep inside he secretly hoped I'd rise above my cloudy angst and make it as a shining player at that game he loved so much.

I think I might take some time out.

He nodded. Inhaled. Replied, *You can always come back to it.*

He was right. I would.

But not until after he died.

A lot is said, written and postulated about teenage male self-esteem. Adolescent males do not tend to perform academically as well as the girls in most co-ed high schools and that log on their shoulders always appears to be getting progressively heavier.

A recent newspaper snippet in *The Canberra Times* entitled 'Structure of Schools to Blame for Boys' Marks' suggests that problems lie first and foremost in the fragile male psyche. The cracks begin to appear when, compared with the girls, boys tend to display poor literacy skills and an inability to communicate effectively except in monosyllabic grunts. Boys are arriving, for reasons unexplained, into the classroom with fewer background skills to cope with 'the higher levels of verbal reasoning' needed to survive these days. Consequently, they resort to disrupting proceedings, perhaps a resourceful tactic to 'deflect the ball', so to speak. As the snippet read,

> 'It is a universal phenomenon that boys, on average, regardless of their socioeconomic backgrounds, are not achieving as well as their female counterparts at all levels of schooling,' Dr Ken Rowe said in the national journal *Boys in Schools Bulletin*... 'What's more, such boys tend to be more alienated and (uninterested) because of the whole nature of the organisation of schooling...' He said that he and his wife, paediatrician Kathy Rowe, had produced strong evidence that boys' poor literacy led to disruptive behaviour, rather than the disruptive behaviour resulting in poor literacy.

It mustn't help that being able to express yourself sensitively and clearly is generally considered by us blokes to be a little nerdy, wimpy and a bit girlish. Besides, we'd rather play video games or watch telly.

A recent Australian Bureau of Statistics study showed that fifty-nine per cent of twelve- to fourteen-year-olds watch twenty hours of television a fortnight (and I don't think we're talking about wildlife documentaries here) and sixty-nine per cent channel their angst through joysticks. In violent computer games, we can express our alienation and disinterest by obliterating aliens and clinically pulverising unfamiliar streetfighters and ninjas that were stupid enough to stray onto our turf. And on top of all this, with incredibly flexible karate chops, we can get hours of exercise for our finger joints. Don't misunderstand me here - I love *Xena* and *Streetfighter*. But they are definitely not helping me evolve my literacy beyond monosyllabic grunting. *Heeeeeeeyaaaaaaa!*

However, there are some refreshing stats. In the same study it was found that fifty-nine per cent of all children played organised sport outside of school hours, away from the lure of Xena and Johnny Big-Balls. So a few boys, at least, were having some structured and essential time of the day left to express themselves without words through *outdoor* games and sport. Allowing time for some of the non-literary, verbally ineffectual males to let off some competitive steam, while simultaneously building confidence and muscle, must do something to help.

But then how did my father with his short, Dutch-accented, grammatically confused sentences and effortless use of silence so strongly command respect and attention and consequently motivate and inspire so many young boys in his lifetime? Could we relate to his very male clumsiness with words? Was it because his expert knowledge, referent power and sincere, quietly confident manner communicated important things very effectively *in spite* of his fumbling to find the correct words at times? (I remember reading a description of the Brazilian coach, Rene Simoes, who took Jamaica to the World Cup Finals in 1998 communicating with an 'inimitable form of broken English, a dialect that relied on hybrid words and lots of body movement' - and felt that this would be a similarly apt way of describing Dad's manner of communication.)

Yet to me the answer is simple and straightforward: he was a *real* human being and he was *around*.

In his excellent paper, *Teaching Social Responsibility*, educator Dr Timothy Hawkes tells of his being alarmed by a *Wall Street Journal* statistic which indicated

> ...that American parents spend less than 15 minutes a week in serious discussion with their children, and for fathers, the amount of close association with their children is 17 seconds a day.

It certainly puts a whole new perspective on the concept

of quality time when you have under twenty seconds for it to occur. I suddenly felt spoilt by those long sunset sessions on Holman Street.

Hawkes then goes on to quote from Steve Biddulph:

> What children get from a career father is not happiness, nor his teaching, nor his substance, but only his mood. And at seven o'clock at night that mood is mostly irritation and fatigue. Men show their love by working hard and long. They do not get appreciated for it – since it is their presence not their bounty that is hungered by their children.

In brief, dads, your children need your presence, not your presents.

It also does not hurt for them to find some good role models somewhere.

A lot has also been said about self-image, heroes and role models. It was, for me at least, imperative that I had successful male figures to look up to, idolise and receive inspiration from in those formative years. As a hip twelve-year-old, I happily marched, make-up on my face and tongue protruding, in the Kiss Army. And after all, it was the big, evil, bass guitarist Gene Simmons who once crooned:

> A world without heroes
> Is like a world without sun

You can't look up to anyone
Without heroes...

(I still think that's pretty cute for someone who spits blood and breathes fire.)

Sure, rock stars, sports stars and actors all featured prominently on my adolescent bedroom wall, along with Supergirl Helen Slater, Princess Caroline of Monaco and Olivia Newton-John carefully woven into the fabric. As Robert Drewe writes in *The Shark Net*,

> I thought I was pretty shrewd back then pasting up the pictures of Brando and the other males as cover and balance for Brigitte, Ava and Marilyn. For about a year not a day had passed when I didn't think of Bardot in *And God Created Woman*. But displaying such come-hither-looking women on their own would have been asking for trouble.

But the adolescent male needs inspiration from real people too. Marlon Brando will never appear, to give him an acting master class; nor lanky Hans van Breukelen pop in at a training session to share some goalkeeping tips; and, sadly, it is no more likely that some sexy super-vixen, princess or rock diva will ever be an option for a formal date. Far away from international sports stadiums, royal palaces and Hollywood glitter, there need to exist more gritty, imperfect but no less influential *human* people in their lives. People who live in the real, everyday surrounds. People who struggle with the same things that they do, week in and week out: the pressures of constantly having to produce the goods and reach expectations; of having to cope with mistakes and errors of judgement that seem insurmountable; of having continually to find inspiration at times when it's absent; of having to recognise and aspire to realistic goals; of having to fight physical and mental barriers in order to achieve these goals; of having to work hard, regularly and incessantly even to keep up with the pacemakers; of having to resist the joys of short-term success over long-term happiness; and, regardless of failures and successes, of having the tenacity to maintain survival on a daily basis with your dignity, integrity and self-confidence intact.

In movies, our heroes mostly succeed in checklisting all of the above in a lifetime of about one and a half hours. Maybe that's why we idolise them. They can do things we normal folk cannot. And in half the time.

In reality, it can take very long, uninspiring and sometimes painful lengths of time to achieve things. This is where good coaches, teachers, leaders and mentors come into their own. They are the constants in their charges' fluctuating allegiances, moods, abilities and desires, showing them ways of making the struggle in small things like sport, and larger things like existence, something well worth working at. In the case of boys in this new millennium, more real, gritty and human inspiration is needed to give them a better start.

With a little more than seventeen seconds to spare.

Recently, I sat myself down with a pile of catch-up videos and seventeen hours a week to spare. The first one I chose was called *Life is Beautiful*, for which its star, director and writer, Roberto Benigni, attracted a lot of attention and praise. I know boys don't cry. But, despite these being enlightened times, what follows is still very hard for me to write dry-eyed. As the end credits of this moving film were scrolling past, I wept. And then wept a little bit more. What was it about that silly movie with its uncertain genre that had struck such a chord in me?

While the world was going crazy around him, murderously war-crazy, the Benigni character tried his damnedest, against impossible odds, to make life in a concentration camp all seem like a game to his son, who was not yet ready to comprehend the enormity of what was happening around him. In the face of incredible adversity, the spectre of anti-Semitism, he managed to remain true to himself as a father and as a fun-loving human citizen. It was clear from the outset that Benigni would always remain his own silly person, even when social, political and historical forces were doing their utmost to bend him.

It would, ultimately, all turn out for the best. Of that he had no doubts. (Cue to Benigni, winking.)

He never, even when it meant making the ultimate sacrifice, compromised his integrity, determination, vitality, sense of humour and perspective, and sheer love of living. These were legacies acknowledged by his son in later life in a voice over at the end of the movie.

I wrote in a poem once that Dad would sometimes '... suck away at the thought – not totally erased by the Germans way back on another, larger rectangle – that he had some bearing on things.' I think, like Benigni, he most certainly did.

When the stakes get high in the silly games that you play, you could always hear Dad mumble, *It's just a game*, those four words bringing you straight back into line with what truly mattered on the field of life. In those moments when you are confused and anxious, the remedy is simple: *Try your best. Then decide.* But, to quote a non-footballing, Elizabethan playwright, *This above all: to thine own self be true.*

In the time I was away from the soccer pitch – that nomadic, uncertain but blissful period between finishing school, going to uni and then eventually finding and settling into a job – at those times when I was distinctly frustrated by things, I would think back on a list of things my Dad said on or near a soccer pitch. Their meanings, of course, lifting off those little paddocks of the past: *Work hard but happily play hard but don't be hard sail through life rather than rage against it give your best but give yourself a break learn by watching others stand up speak up then shut up talent exists in the most unlikely of places remember training try to hang onto it whenever you can try your best then decide it's up to you it's just a game you can always come back to it enjoy what you're doing or do something else know when genoeg is genoeg...*

I see him turning gently away, walking into the mist of memory, a small orb of orange light glowing from the cigarette between his fingers.

It was these words which probably lingered in the subconscious and helped to eventually reactivate my interest in soccer. And they ultimately led me to know when the time came to close the curtain. At least, a decade after his death, Jan – sorry, *John* – Huitker's son can safely write that his father's words got through to him and yes, indeed, they have had a rather significant bearing on things. Not just footy, I might add.

I remember back to the Dutch national team finally winning something big and Allan Border bowling surprisingly well. Stranger things can happen.

And do.

My Father's Last Stand

Firstly, there was the cricket.
That test against the Windies:
a victory against everything.

Thrilled,
we followed each delivery
with forced and tender breath.

You told me,
Border should bowl
more often. He underrates himself.

I imagine those bedridden
moments next to the woman
you loved; Mum

close as dignity,
straightening everything:
bed, pillows, linen.

Then in the morning, with the newspaper
I'd slip contraband –
a bar of white chocolate

like cigarettes
in the schoolyard.
Hide it in the drawer, Dad.

(We'd done this for years –
gentle, irreverent bucks
to the system.)

And the day before you died –
when you left
as if on a business trip –

I sat by your bed, nervous
for my first day of work.
You were content

that I was *finally going*
to do something I loved
that paid, to boot!

I passed the hospital today;
construction cordons,
cranes,
and cables like drips.
Like a bloody prison.
True, Dad,

but would you
have sacrificed
our last-wicket stand

and not faced the last ball?
You knew that a game
can be won

off the final delivery.

2. The Second Half: Not Just a Premiership

I can take a bad game from a player – but I cannot take a dishonest one.
– Gordon Strachan, *Staying Up*, 1997

I remember turning to Matthew at some point during the 1998 season and saying, *This is really getting out of hand now.*

In 1996, my Under 13 Division 2 soccer team won their premiership. It was the first time I could ever remember coming first or, to be more precise, being directly associated with anything coming first.

Buoyed by my first ever premiership win as a coach, I thought I was going to be Canberra's answer to Alex Ferguson, and decided to take it all so much further the following year. However, I had very little reason to be quite that confident. I was certainly not challenging Terry Venables for a job with the national side. Confused by the football logic, patterns, technics, skills and philosophy I was asked to consume at my Level Two Coaching course in 1997, I inelegantly bombed out.

My attitude did not help. Being surrounded by a herd of English and Scottish accents also did not help. Why was it that everybody I seemed to come across in any position of footballing authority in this country was some failed quasi-professional from Europe who had come to Australia hell-bent on saving the ignorant scofflaws from crudely kicking echidnas around dusty paddocks under the shade of koala-filled eucalypts?

I remember vividly the point when I cracked. Our Chelsea-loving, teacher-distrusting, pseudo-mystic, hundred-year-old Head Coach had got me pumping about seventy crosses between two orange witches' hats in order that a colleague – the then Canberra Cosmos pony-tailed hard man, P.J. Roberts – could instruct the fine art of 'crossing to score'. I still get cramps in that leg four years later.

This was followed by a penetrating discussion on what you would do if you had a talented, potential Harry Kewell in your club side. One of the sycophantic Scots on my left said, *Yoo moost let the laddie go on tu bigga n betta things, lika reproosentitive fuuutball. It's soo importn't tu luke afta the well-bean of the tull'n'ted jung players.*

What a load of malarkey.

I suggested that you should keep tull'n'ted young Harry Kewell for yourself, not let him know about the rep trials and try to squeeze a premiership or two out of 'the laddie' before you lost him to the wicked rep coaches or a rival club with snazzy tracksuits. I mean, after all, isn't that what any ambitious junior coach would do if tempted by the horned freak on the left shoulder? Sadly, you cannot always trust the dubious intentions of those in power in junior sport and you also need to consider the 'well-bean' of the rest of your team.

For instance, in a sport where a club coach was the state coach *as well*, that coach could be empowered to select 'the jung laddie' for the state team. He could then 'encourage' the laddie to play with his (the coach's) *club* side in order for the player to form a better bond and connection with his newer, niftier rep peers who also happen to play with that club. Could that be a reason why top club sides seem always to boast a disproportionate plethora of state representatives? And what about the bond and connection formed with 'old' mates from the 'old' club who were callously left behind for his better interests? Is *their* development not worthy of encouragement because they can't make the *top* grade? Surely they would develop significantly with stronger, skilled players alongside them?

In short, a way must be found to make sure that representative players are sprinkled evenly throughout the clubs or a sport could become as boring and predictable as the English Premier League where a Manchester United victory is about as exciting as reading *Middlemarch* in a dentist's waiting room. Quite frankly, in junior sport, competitions and tournaments must not exist solely as training games for representative outfits.

Did I see a few people shift uneasily?

I quit.

If sport does anything for young people, it teaches them about winning and losing (and drawing) and how to cope with each. Not wishing to state the blatantly obvious, there are plenty of times in life when we win, lose and draw. The grace with which we deal with these must obviously be gained through experience. Thus, in our formative years, we observe quite keenly the manner in which our idols, peers, parents and coaches deal with these situations.

For the first few years of my coaching at Radford College (where I have taught and coached since 1989), my sides got to study, quite extensively, the art of Coping With Loss. In some ways, being a coach of losing sides is quite liberating. Free from the expectation of success, you can blissfully remain cheerful and optimistic because ironically you have nothing to lose: *OK, kids, maybe that* wasn't our best performance. But keep your heads up. Let's look to improve and be positive about things. How do you feel we can avoid another 27–0 loss? I know. I'll shout the team a Coke each next week if we can let in under ten.

For most kids, the lure of sugar or a trip to Maccas is often enough to fix flayed spirits. But as they get older, it does get harder, that's for sure. They become less convinced by saccharine promises with a side order of fries.

It wasn't until – to give myself a change of scenery – I coached my first girls' side in 1995, that I found myself a team who made it into the top half of a draw. As most hadn't played before, I was armed with barrels of patience and ready to gently start from scratch – to begin with the basics – in order to get them close to winning a game or two throughout the inaugural season. As the perceptive Belgian coach Robert Waseige once said, *We have to improve in two key areas – defence and attack.*

I remember saying to my little ladies just before kick off at our first game, *I want you to go out there and do your best. I want you to know that winning isn't everything. Let's go out there and learn a little about the game and about each other, as well as making it hard for the opposition to score goals. But remember – just do your best. I can't ask for any more than that. A win or two this season would be a great achievement.*

After winning our first match and remaining undefeated until Round Four, my tone had changed somewhat: *Girls, it is very possible for us to finish in the top three this year. I know it's only our first season together, but we need to capitalise on our leads when we hit the front – and give that little bit extra in order to hold onto a win. I mean it all adds up at the end of the season. I know most of you are trying your best, but I need you to dig deep and give that little bit extra. That's what winning sides do. Finishing third or higher would be a great achievement.*

It was obvious my ego had grown that little bit *extra*.

The girls finished fourth that year, with everyone ecstatic about how much we had evolved as players and people throughout a happy year together. The girls' confidence and my ego weren't the only things that grew bigger that year. Mum's Sideline Café was in full swing, attracting each team member's parent (and sometimes opposition folk too) to our little Radford huddle week in and week out despite work obligations, the weather and other conflicting adult interests. Some parents even confessed to coming solely for the social scene that mother's blossoming canteen had attracted. This has always been her gift.

Not that she's ever known when to stop.

Jeane's Sideline Café became bigger than Marlon Brando.

With a range of coffees, teas, biscuits, chocolates and enough confectionery to have your whole team spewing by ten minutes into the second half (Jeane was banned from feeding players jelly snakes during the break), I felt at one point the need to remind the parents that their girls were actually playing some pretty good soccer a few metres away on the playing fields. But it was hard to get too pompous about it all. Mum was, after all, assuming Dad's role on the sidelines, week in and week out, bringing people together in her own polystyrene style.

The following year, the gals finished second, pipped at the post by a classy Tuggeranong side stacked with state reps who had been playing soccer since they leapt out of the cot juggling a soccer ball. There's always one, isn't there? One big blessed hurdle stuck between you and that fairy tale finish. But, I said to myself, let's get real here. Two years ago hardly any of the girls had played soccer before. And here they were, one spot away from immortality. When I bump into these young ladies now, often on their way to and from university or in shopping centres or getting ready for weddings, I don't think there's a single one of them who doesn't fondly remember every ball happily kicked to the smell of strong Dutch coffee.

It was here, with these darling little ladies, that the first signs of soccer psychosis began to rear its ugly head. When you have a losing side, wins are fantastic and unexpected delights. You are also used to losing and able to lose. When you are on a winning side, wins are expected and all sense of fantasy or delight is diminished. You also become unwilling and in some cases unable to lose.

That's when you need to watch yourself.

Let me see. George. Blondie. Keysie. Nattie. Nijie. Scotty. Frenchie. Fifers. Cuth. Jimmy. Chris. Mark. Azza. And Jon, late as always. (In four years' time he'd still be missing the bus, this time in Manchester at the other end of the world. Some things never change.) These were the boys who made the first Under 13 cut in 1996 and in doing so won the dubious privilege of playing for their school in second division.

How was I going to sell that to my class players? Second division. Especially when some of them would easily be able to play Division 1 for a local club. That was something Radford had never yet been able to do – place a competitive team in the junior first division. And it really irked me.

In the summer of that year, I had seen the potential of some of the younger boys on Year 7 Camp at Illaroo Farm, Nowra, where across a cowpat-spattered lopsided paddock (which later would remind me of half the fields we played on in England in 2000) a few lively lads could not resist exhibiting their skills for the girls on the slopes in a 'friendly' before dinner one afternoon. Despite the sudden undulations, which could find the unwary participant disappear ball and all into some trench on the playing field then reappear further down with a cowpat beret on his head, it was evident that we had a better proportion of dexterous players than in years past.

I rushed back to Radford to tell Mark, the 1995 Under 13 side's captain. Mark was still eligible to play Under 13s again in 1996 and was a curly-haired, natural leader sort of kid. He had the distinction of captaining one of the most hopeless teams I've ever coached in my life. The '95ers, which I coached in conjunction with my girls' team, were diverse lads of all shapes and sizes and skill levels and we had a lot of fun together. But the concept of winning was going to be as foreign to them as Diego Maradona.

And speaking of foreign, scanning down my team list all I could really find was one Greek and one Croatian surname. And definitely no Argentines. This never bodes well for success in soccer. I suppose, if I threw my surname in, we could add a Dutch connection, but that might forever cast some gloomy spell on the team which would see them coming close but never really achieving anything for the rest of existence.

Whatever the case, I stood in front of them at the end of the first training and found my mouth driving in automatic: *Don't worry about being in Division 2. You're all better than Division 2. But we need to prove it. We can't just walk into Division 1. Things don't work like that. So let's just mentally readjust and see Division 2 as a confidence-building exercise. We'll build the squad's camaraderie and consolidate skills along the way. Then, after we win the competition, next season we'll be promoted into Division 1, where we'll truly be ready to really show 'em what we can do! Are you with me, boys?*

YEAH! screeched my fifteen thirteen-year-olds as if they were about to follow William Wallace into the fray.

Those little tykes left that first training, God bless their little souls, with their premiership trophies already shining on their mantelpiece. I left wondering why I have never been able to control my very very big big mouth.

To date, I had never played in, let alone coached, a team that had finished in the top half of a draw – with the glittering exception of my little ladies who had now disappeared into the great soccer-hereafter of rep squads, Women's Soccer, part-time jobs, deep and meaningful relationships and other unsportly interests.

I needn't have worried. In that 1996 season, the boys scored over one hundred goals and conceded just over ten. It was a for-and-against that no other Radford side had ever approached and one of our first premierships in the ACT Junior League. Within a year, we were heading for the majors.

Going into Division 1, I thought that all the players who had snubbed us in 1996 would see the error of their ways and come over and patriotically play for their school. Only two did: Matthew from the Junior Giants, Belnorth Gold, and Drew, a goalkeeper from Belnorth Blue – the blossoming club's second first division team.

Around this time in the English Premier League, Gordon Strachan assumed control of Coventry City Football Club from Ron Atkinson. I have long been a fan of Gordon Strachan, a coach famous for his hate-hate relationship with referees who, in his eyes, could never conceivably get anything right, even if you paid them. The fiery Scot could be angry at referees for global warming, Third World famine and the Great Depression *on top of* poor refereeing decisions. And that's even after a Coventry win.

But it was Strachan's unrelenting passion for the game that was inspirational to me. Despite the fact that

Coventry would never make the top half of the Premier League ladder and would always be blessed with only being able to afford the most professionally mediocre of football players, he would never let this affect his drive and high expectations for the club. They had, after all, been in the top flight since 1967, the year I was born. (Distressingly, as I write, this dogged tenancy appears to be coming to an end.)

Strachan's parents were also at one stage concerned about his psychological well-being (as most British footballing parents should be), but an undaunted Gordie confidently replied, *I am passionate and I was like that as a player, but I'm not doing anyone any harm. I might be doing myself harm... I just can't contain it. My dad and mum have had a word with me about it, so I had a check-up a few weeks ago and I'm a perfectly formed specimen. Small but perfectly formed – I'm very relaxed.*

You gotta love this guy. I often wondered how Gordie Strachan would approach Under 14 Division 1. In my shoes he probably would've thought, *Bloody typical. You work your way into the major league and get enough money to sign two measly players. Oh well, better make them count...*

In many ways, at many times in 1997, I felt I could relate a lot to Strachan. Like Coventry, I wanted to keep my lads playing at the top level, maintain some pride in their play and not do anything that would see them relegated back to the lower divisions. If they made the top half of the draw, that would be fantastic. A bonus even.

Like Gordon, I became immensely fiery. And with each loss it became worse. There were plenty of them stacking up. I would get angry when I saw Radford students who had decided they would not play for their school lining up in opposition sides. I would get angry when referees did not understand how hard we tried and gave the oppositions, who were invariably beating us, free bloody kicks. I got angry when opposition coaches belittled our crappy school outfit. That always motivated me and the boys.

By the halfway point of the season, it seemed their choice to play elsewhere had been justified. We had only managed two wins and a draw and a forgettable run of losses. Some matches were very close and it often felt that Lady Luck was never totally on our side. I remember what Jimmy Connors used to say – that the harder he worked the luckier he became. I remember telling the boys this. They would look at me flummoxed and ask me who the hell was Jimmy Connors.

Despondent, I remember saying to Matthew's mother, Jenny-May, that I could understand she may be disappointed in having switched allegiances from

Matthew's old team, Belnorth Glittering Gold. (Even goalkeeper Drew's old team, the second-string Belnorth Blue, had daintily placed balls past their old 'keeper – something that must have been hard for Drew to swallow.) Belnorth Glorious Gold were leading the competition, chock-a-block full of State reps, and hadn't looked like losing a game in the last fifty seasons. Jenny-May replied that Matthew was learning more from this losing side than he ever had at Belnorth. Finally allowed to wander out of the backline, where he usually never saw the ball at all, he was now in the midfield at Radford, playing a leadership role and forced to work creatively and regularly in order to develop as a player with his new team. I could have kissed her.

But decisions, close calls and matches never seemed to go our way. I worked like a Trojan to keep my boys buoyant and persistent, striving harder to break the drought. I even photocopied for the lads Winston Churchill's famous speech before the House of Commons on 4 June 1940 upon the surrendering of the Belgian army to the German war machine. (The Belgians obviously had to work on defence and attack during WWII as well.)

> We shall go on to the end...
> We shall fight on the seas and oceans...
> We shall defend our island whatever the cost may be...
> We shall never surrender.

We most certainly would never surrender. If there's one thing I can infuse in young soldiers, it is a bit of militant self-pride. But the losses kept dumping down on us from a great height and the costs and casualties became greater.

And then the sideline café had to close for the season. Mum went and had a heart attack.

I can remember sitting in the waiting room at Woden Valley Hospital wondering who would look after the team on the weekend. At least Mum had her heart attack on a Wednesday, leaving me time to organise someone to look after the team in their big match against Belnorth.

The nurse, disturbing my thoughts, said, *Your mother's had a minor heart attack. She'll need to go to Sydney for an angioplasty – probably tonight by helicopter. She's very tired and mustn't be disturbed for too long...*

Ashamed, I looked at her there on the bed, reverberations of seeing Dad in a similarly vulnerable position eight years earlier running through my head. And then her eyes caught mine and I can remember feeling terrified that maybe she had seen that screen inside my head – all those thoughts of 'what if' demanding to be played out through to the dreaded final reel.

Even if she did see inside it, we both knew that Jeane was tougher than anything a clogged artery could throw at her. She had that look of exhausted calm that people sometimes have after something bad has happened to them. As Bob Mould once sang, *To watch it all collapsing in some strange way is so relaxing.* And there was also that glint of unselfish Jeane Huitker concern for others from which no calamity could distract her.

She apologised for disturbing me at school. And asked if I had had to cancel training.

By the end of the month, all the Under 14 Division 1 team had paid her a visit, written her a letter or sent her flowers. And promised that they'd do something in their cloudy soccer season to see a little light.

A whole round of fixtures had passed since Mum's heart attack and we found ourselves facing the mighty Belnorth Gargantuan Gold for the second time. With its premiership flag firmly in its pocket they came to Radford with every intention to give us a pummelling and to remind us that the 3–1 result earlier in the year was a flattering aberration. Who did Radford think they were to even think to resist that day? The Belnorth Gleaming Gold team were still, of course, yet to lose a game of soccer since woolly mammoths roamed the plains.

I read around this time in an article in *The Canberra Times* that pre-match pep talks were a waste of breath. A London sports psychologist, Stephen Smith believed,

> Many football coaches did not have the time to really understand their players, and angry rants or impassioned speeches had no influence on the outcome of a match. He said that failures at training cannot be compensated for in the dressing room.

Well, all I could say to Dr Smith, Will Robinson and their trusty Robot is that, hey, I've made a career of it. And I bet Gordon Strachan has too. Na na dee na na.

If Stephen Smith had been there when I spoke pre-match to my charges I'm sure he would have changed his thesis. Our trainings had been getting progressively sloppy – they were failures, if you like – but after a season of essentially turning losing into a lifestyle, perseverance and inspiration to improve were all we really had left. Besides, like the Belgians, we had only two key areas to work on – defence and attack. And I had paid a small fortune in lollies and chocolates to keep spirits from drooping.

I have a vague recollection of the content of my pep talk (and you can use it any time you need it, Stephen): *They have no right to come here and assume you are easy-beats. They have no right to assume they are better than you. They have no right to think that winning is a certainty. Nothing is certain – I've learned that much this year. Now, let's give them a taste of what losing feels like. We know it. And we also know we've had enough. Don't win this for me, boys. Or for Mum. Or your school. Win it for yourself. The good guys gotta win sometime.*

The boys gave a roar straight out of *Braveheart* which in turn gave me an unsettling feeling of déjà vu. A shaft of sunlight beamed through the grey clouds as an orchestra started playing somewhere and the wind blew my hair majestically sideways like the Bee Gees on the cover of *Spirits Having Flown*. Their roar echoed across Gossan Hill where the kangaroos stopped munching, momentarily, and sensed something electric in the air.

We won the game 3–0.

I've never known a better win in my soccer life.

In the way that cheeky bottom-placed teams can sometimes do, we had taken and tarnished a little bit of the premiers' glory and made it our own.

For a change, we felt like winners and I couldn't wait to get to Jeane and tell her as much.

Then came 1998.

I can remember sitting in a Year 9 classroom waiting for my prospective Under 15 Division 1s to arrive for a preliminary meeting and nearly keeling over in my chair in shock when two members of the Belnorth Glimmering Gold Machine, Jono and Matt (who referred to himself as Giggs and/or Big Nuts), walked in and took a seat. Both had just returned from a successful tour of Japan with an Australian futsal side and were regular starters for the ACT Under 15 rep team. Surely they had come to the meeting to mock.

Also present was a dexterous, jolly-natured, robust blond kid the boys affectionately called 'Fattie' who had played in yet another invincible premiership-winning outfit with a younger Belnorth side. Despite being a year younger, he was friendly with all of my team members and, despite the distinct possibility of experiencing the new sensation of losing, had decided he'd rather play with his mates at the school. I wish more young people followed his example.

After organising the first training and being careful not to give away any of my secrets on how to finish third last on the table, I asked Jono and Big Nuts to remain behind and chew cud, uncertain of their intentions. I thanked them for showing an interest in what we were doing at Radford and inquired how they thought they'd do in '98.

Oh, we'll win it, said Big Nuts.

You must be pretty used to that over at Belnorth, I replied.

No, we'll win it with Radford. We're signing up for Radford, Big Nuts confidently returned.

That's nice, I stammered while my fingers were drumming a nervous beat on the teacher's chair. Collecting myself, I clasped my hands together in front of my fly like a defender standing in the wall and said, with a studied, ice-cool nonchalance, *Well, I'll see you both at training on Tuesday.*

I wanted to ask them why they had a change of heart, colours and team. Did it have anything to do with that match last year? Did they like what they saw was happening with soccer at Radford? Did they want to share more than just calculus with their classmates? But I couldn't find it within myself to ask those questions.

As they walked out the door, I waved, daggily. Ryan Giggs and Eric Cantona had just told me they wanted to leave Manchester United and play for Coventry City. They were willing to leave their top-placed, rep-stacked shimmering side to join the ranks of grey and maroon cellar-dwellers.

For all of the previous year I had moaned about how, if I had all the potential Division 1 players in my school side, we'd show the world a thing or two. This was an easy thing to moan about, especially in the relative security that it was something that was as likely to happen as a female pope. And now it had.

So, for about the millionth time in my soccer coaching life, my big big mouth had put my small small credentials right into the firing line. What the blazes was I going to do now?

I spent many nights neglecting my teacherly duties of lesson prep and marking, shunning the real world in favour of ethereal sporting possibilities, and preferring to focus my energies on my newly bolstered team. I contacted every coach and soccer mentor I even vaguely knew, extracting anecdotes, wisdom and experiences as well as training manuals, magazines and books on tactics, nutrition and wisdom, and even useless things like a two-volume set of *Dutch Training Drills*.

I became fascinated if not somewhat obsessed by a video I found, curiously titled *The Creative Dribbler*, in which these precocious little soccer brats from Qatar exhibited, with effortless ease, some phenomenally confusing soccer drills designed to make them – well, dribble better. I watched these little Mozarts of football for hours on end, marvelling at the way they intuitively and instinctively showcased an array of complex skills and drills. I had to rewind the tape sixty times to comprehend them even slightly and then transcribe the drills, through a complex system of diagrams and arrows, into my Olympic striped exercise book (which I hadn't opened since the Level Two Coaching course debacle). It was *hard work*.

So I arrived at that first training ready to impress the old and new boys with a range of fantastic skills I had picked up from some extensive off-season study of internationally renowned techniques and tactics. After being with the boys for two years, I knew I had to offer them something with a little more variety and challenge than the 'kicking-down-the-witches'-hats', 'fox-and-hound', 'keepings-off', 'two-on-two-in-the-box-plus-goalie', the ever popular 'soccer-volleyball' hybrid or the 'tired' and true 'take-potshots-at-the-goalie-for-two-hours' option. (Players love this and will do it for days without food and water.)

It was a debacle. The players couldn't understand my instructions let alone the drill and I kept soldiering on like those fish that swim up waterfalls. I had chosen Niagara Falls to swim up. *What's the point of all this?* a different team member would ask me every three seconds or so and I'd petulantly reply, *Well, maybe we'd be less easy-beats if we actually developed our skills a little instead of wanting to take potshots at Drew or dicking around playing soccer-volleyball every single bloody training. It would be nice to win a game or two every now and then. It would be nice to develop our match play beyond kicking it up to the forwards with a hopeful giggle and a pirouette. So if you want to play in the starting line-up for the first game this weekend you'll shut up and do it and get skilful and develop and improve, damn you.*

I have no idea what Jono and Big Nuts were thinking about this eloquent spontaneously combusting coach with his bizarre and bewildering combination of drills possibly more intricate than anything they received from their national coaches. (Or later from their teachers in Senior Physics.) Thankfully, as they were new, they smiled politely and tried to work it all out for themselves.

Whatever the case, by the halfway point of training, with balls flying everywhere, every player scratching his head and Mark serenely informing me that it wasn't really working all that well but it was nice that I was trying to do something different, I threw my hands to the sky and said, *Play a game of soccer-volleyball then, while I study my diagrams.*

As I increased my headache by trying to decipher my own stick-figure representation of something akin to relativity theory, the boys happily organised themselves into two teams, put out the witches' hats and proceeded to play. I was about to yell at them for laughing too loudly when I actually looked up from my shorthand hieroglyphics and noticed the boys smiling and, with a strangely happy-serious combination of intensity and concentration, practise all the skills and drills that I had previously and successfully failed to transmute into a mind-bogglingly complex sequence of activities. They were using their head, chest, thigh and feet in a myriad of ways to control, lay off, pass and kick the ball to each other; becoming increasingly aware of their use of space and what they were doing 'off the ball'; developing a craftiness, sneakiness and team cohesion in order to win points; and varying the style, pace and shape of their game play at every turn. And they were laughing while they did all this. Having fun.

Years later, a friend gave me an article by John Webb in an *XY* magazine feature on men and sport which reminded me of this little episode. Writes Webb,

> The perception of sport from which I still suffer after all those years of training in adolescence is that sport is somehow work; that I need to create around it the same mystique and aura of the sacred that protects the time I allot to work; and that I need to commit myself to sport with the same degree of fanaticism I bring to other activities in which I engage the details without considering the process or its endpoint.

And here was I, quite intentionally, turning my soccer trainings into my work, making it a classroom with diagrams and overheads which all went well and truly over the players' heads anyway. Here I was at the first training of the year bringing textbooks of tactics instead of lollies and a sense of adventure and excitement.

I turned around and there was William Shakespeare, sitting on my kit, looking out pensively at the lads at play. He looked at my Olympic striped exercise book and made a big farty condescending sound with his lips, then said,

> Raze out the written troubles of the brain, Georgie. Throw physic to the dogs. I'll none of it. These giddy drills and sweet oblivious antidotes to losing, being told by an idiot, are full of sound and fury, signifying nothing. You numbskull, to thine own self be true. If I chance to talk a little wild, forgive me; I had it from thy father...

I blinked. And where Shakespeare had spread his Elizabethan posterior was a trusty packet of jelly snakes Jeane had sneaked into the kit bag for the boys. (She frequently planted these subversive treats where the boys would find them and I might not.)

We finished the training with some shots at the goalies. I gave the snakes out with a sigh as the boys were leaving. The lads, in a typical adolescent way, had been expecting them, devoured them as if they hadn't been fed in weeks, then took off to their cars complaining that I'd only brought one packet.

Luckily, I had been too stunned by the clinical, consistent and casual manner with which Big Nuts had been finishing goals during the final session to give them all a lecture on teenage egocentricity. It looked as though scoring goals was what Big Nuts did in his sleep. (This was something he was to continue to do on weekends.)

As I passed the rubbish hopper on my way to the car after training, I threw my Olympic striped exercise book into it as Big Nuts, walking behind me said, *It's not as intense as rep training but, gee, it's more fun. We're going to do well this year. We've got some good players here. At least top three, guarantee it.*

Despite the positive signs, I'd been burned too much in the past as a player and fan of Dutch soccer. I had my doubts. Naturally good natured and skilled as these boys were, if I couldn't teach them – let alone comprehend myself – the elite and advanced skills needed to be a 'creative dribbler', surely I wouldn't be able to make my new and improved team reach anywhere near its potential.

One of the most painful things I had to do in 1998 was

cut the squad. It had grown too big. Unfortunately, a few of my players hadn't. Working out who to cut was not all that difficult – it was *telling* them that was gut-wrenching. One hyperkinetic kid in particular had not been able to mix it with the larger and more skilful oppositions over the last season in Under 14s. That I had grown quite fond of this eccentric little guy with a strange tendency to tune out during trainings and begin spontaneous, aerobic air karate with invisible ninjas, made it all the more sickening to my stomach. The fact remained that, while he always walked over the bad guys in his head, he struggled to make it happen in reality on the soccer pitch.

I remember how I felt nearly twenty years earlier when I was left behind by my buddy Sean. I remember having no understanding of how the adults in charge could be so short-sighted and so lacking in any awareness of how I felt about what was going on. I knew how these boys would feel. They'd hate me forever. I would too if I was in their shoes. Boots. Whatever.

I pulled them aside at school during the week and told them, one on one, that I had to drop them from the team. I left Ninjaboy until last. When I called him over I could see in his eyes he knew what it was about and, in his amazing, unsentimental, dignified way, he opened the conversation with, *I know what you're going to say. I know what's coming. The second I saw those new players walk in that room to sign up I knew it'd be me that would have to make way.*

(Pause.) *Are you angry about it?*

No, H. It was good while it lasted. I got to win a premiership two years ago. That was rad.

I haven't slept all week, you know. Telling you this news is the hardest thing I've ever had to do as a coach.

Sure, H.

It is. Please believe that.

You do what you gotta do, H.

You going to give up soccer? I hope you d–

I don't really want to play in Division 2 without my friends. I think I'll take some time out.

He walked away from me. And I knew he was walking away from the game as well. To my knowledge, he never kicked a soccer ball or an invisible ninja again.

If my father had been the coach here and now he would have found some way to make it work – squeeze eighteen bodies into a squad of fifteen. He was a magician like that. I was a fraud. A great big faker.

By the halfway point of the season we were undefeated.

Big Nuts just kept scoring goals from all ends of the
field. I remember one game where a coach/parent
(which, as we all know, is a potentially awful situation)
was bragging how *his* goalie/son was the best 'keeper
on the planet as well as the ACT and *he* had connections
with Bosnich and *his* son was going to play in the
Premier League before the boy so much as sported facial
hair. I'll give that coach/parent this much – his boy was
good and managed to keep us goalless for most of the
game. In a tense finale, well into the second half of the
second half, Big Nuts sent a thunderbolt flying from
near the halfway line, a la Stephen Larkham, which
whizzed past Bosnich into the top corner of the net.
We won 1–0. Now, had that father not gloated *quite* so
much, I would have probably accepted the win with
some quiet dignity. But within earshot of the opposition
coach I felt hopelessly (and pathetically) compelled to
applaud Drew for keeping a clean sheet for the match
and promised him a future keeping goals in England
if he stuck with *me*.

From that day, I tried with determination not to refer
to the team as 'mine', at least not publicly. Was this
silly? I felt that to claim ownership of the boys was like
claiming to have been a lifelong fan of the Raiders, but
only after they won the 1989 Grand Final. To boast that

the boys were 'my team' also placed an unnecessary and unearned stress on the fact that I was their coach and hence, as possession is nine-tenths of the law, I had something to do with their success. I honestly felt that all that I was really doing was shaping some pretty malleable play dough, which someone else had baked, into my own nifty, unconventional end product. That I actually had something to do with their *success* was quite impossible for me to accept. I was, after all, a supporter of the Dutch national side and doomed to wreck things. And besides, I'd seen enough yukky stuff come from coaches living vicariously through their players to know that I didn't want to go down that road. I didn't know much about creative dribbling, but I knew that much.

I can say with some truth that, as the wins kept piling up, I tried to remain as quiet and unassuming as possible. I could see the oppositions' coaches frequently eyeing us off during our warm-ups – a bizarre combination of drills I stole from Dad, the Level Two debacle, other coaches and what my rep players informed me worked for them at ACT training. Whereas I used to go up and happily shake hands with opposition coaches during these warm-ups and say *Welcome to Radford – try to keep your score to single-digit numbers*, I now just said, *Welcome to Radford*, which must have sounded a little like *Hi, I'm Satan! Welcome to my fire pit...*

And then, of course, there were the ever-present opposition pohwnis. Some were rather abrupt and rude at times. *The only reason you're winning is you coerced those players to leave their clubs and forced them to play for you.* (I'd look at my team warming up metres away, often to see Big Nuts, Jono, Fattie, Drew or Matthew wrestling with and/or mooning each other while deliriously cackling like a pack of second-graders.)

It was around this time I began to realise that pohwnis actually speak in a different language from humans and really need subtitles like you get on SBS World Movies. For example:

i) *Radford play dirty now* and *It's not rugby, Radford!* meant that Radford no longer lets itself get pushed around. (They wouldn't correlate anything to rugby if they saw some of our First XV's score lines of late.)

ii) *Radford only has one Division 1 team performing well* meant that the opposition had just lost to the only Radford side in the Junior League which had the audacity *not* to let itself be bottom placed in Division 1.

iii) *Give it to 'em – they're nothin'* meant Radford was dominating due to determined and creative play.

iv) *See! They are nothin'* meant that the opposition had just scored a consolation goal to make the score line something like 1–6.

v) *It'll be a different story next time* meant that we had just won the game.

vi) *The ref was shit* meant that we had just won the game.

vii) *Their luck can't last* meant that we had just won the game.

viii) *We'll see how tough you are in the car park after the game* meant that we had just won the game.

ix) *They play boring kick-and-chase English-style* meant that Big Nuts scored a lot of goals using his pace to outrun the defence. (It also implied that the English play rather speculative soccer.)

x) *Who is that Asian guy anyway?* meant that they were threatened by a coach from a global region who knew more about cooking chow mien than winning soccer games.

It was uncharacteristic of me, but I actually took a leaf out of Dad's book and kept quiet and walked away from these sort of jibes. I was as amazed as others were over the team's success. Although they had a long way to go, the boys were starting to mature a little and not be fazed by being the top team. Sure they enjoyed winning, but as Frenchie's dad pointed out on many occasions throughout the season, *they enjoy each other's company more than any victory.*

I recall replying to him, *Well, even if they don't win another game this season, they behave like a team coached by my father – happy to just be playing – and that's enough for me.*

Mr French'd shake his head with incredulity and murmur, *They'll win the premiership.*

As a matter of fact, the only person not maturing or remaining quite unfazed about being the top team was me. I was just waiting for the crunch to come. Life is not like this. It doesn't allow a welcome run of wins without exacting some nasty little payback or disillusionment.

So I started to will a tragedy.

I didn't need to will too much longer.

Before the mid-year holidays, we lost to rivals Marist in the quarter-finals of the ACT region of the Bill Turner Cup due to a golden goal in extra time. It was our first major disappointment of the season. The boys had been playing good soccer and were expecting to progress interstate in the competition. I was more than a little concerned when the boys were totally inconsolable after the loss. Being around them post-match made standing in the middle of a morgue a far jollier proposition. I remember feeling very inadequate at that point, never having had to counsel winners on how to cope with a surprise loss before. *C'mon, fellers, you can't win 'em all. Heads up!*

I had decided not to play the boys in the Kanga Cup over the holidays (a decision I repeated in 2000) in order to give them a break from soccer. Much as they obviously loved the game, I felt it was a time for them to recreate and pursue other interests like travel, reading, philately or croquet.

Then, over the holidays, Jono severely damaged the crucio-ligament in his left knee playing in the Kanga Cup with the ACT Under 15 side (in an older age group). He would need surgery that would put him out for the rest of the season. Alongside captain Mark in the central defence, Jono had given the team renewed confidence and self-belief. Players like Keysie and Frenchie were playing the most solid and secure defensive games I had ever seen from them. We had the best defence in the competition and scoring a goal against us, as in the Bill Turner quarter-final, tended only to occur when an uncharacteristic error was made. So, when Jono called me and said he had some bad news, I knew already what he'd say next. I don't believe in sporting fairy tales. I was waiting for something to rain on our parade.

One of our early matches in the second half of the season was against the Australian Institute of Sport women's side, which thankfully wasn't worth competition points, but was still played with 'competitive spirit'. (Were two more contradictory words ever put together?) Their coach, an astute thick-accented man – another participant from the Level Two debacle – had me and my boys' match plan sussed. (I actually didn't have a match plan but he was so good he knew what it was.) Controlling possession and tightly 'man-marking' our boys saw the AIS madams dominate and eventually win the game 2–1. My mid-adolescent boys were truly not ready for the amorous attentions their backsides received from the ladies of the opposition and our 'show no respect for the opposition' motto came completely asunder when we incorrectly assumed a pre-programmed gentlemanli-ness that these ferals from the AIS did not deserve or desire. That day marked the death of political correctness in my mind.

Those women were good. Their passing game was superb. But nothing beat their sense of the dramatic and, as a Drama teacher, I would know. I remember seeing an AIS midfielder take an acrobatic tumble which, even to biased ol' me, looked like a blatant foul by one of my players. And this was even after the most casual observer would have registered that the Radford player was in fact a metre – if not a mile – away from where the incident must have occurred. Thus, after completing the tumble, landing on her feet with arms neatly splayed (to which we all held up placards with scores out of ten), this sly AIS thespian completed another forward roll and a Viennese waltz while all the time complaining about the sorry state of women's rights in the nineties and the pain she had received from some crude caveman's slide-tackle. Needless to say, she got the free kick and we got a yellow card.

I noticed as she played the ball the cheekiest, fattest, most truly sinister smirk appear on her cute, clever face.

In the return match against 'Bosnich and Co' (who were having a dream run and closing the gap on us at the top of the table), we found ourselves away from home and 2–0 down at half-time. Once again, I had to call on knowledge I did not have in order to find something useful to motivate my boys, who simply weren't used to being caught in a rut after winning games effortlessly only weeks earlier.

As it was a deferred Sunday fixture, no referees showed up (they were all at church) and I subsequently had to decline the offers of every parent from the opposition's ranks to officiate. A more neutral and qualified referee was found and the game commenced. But the boys, caught in a downward spiral, became flustered by bizarre decisions (hell, I haven't got used to them after two and a half decades in the game) and were easy prey to intimidation from people, pohwnis and players both on and off the field. Two players came off at half-time with bad injuries, one maturely refusing to play for the rest of the game because the ref was a big cheat, another understandably in tears because an opposition parent had hurled personal and abhorrent abuse at him from the opposite side of the pitch, and the remainder looking like a platoon of extras from *The Thin Red Line*.

I knew this was a crunch time and this game could make or break the season. If there was ever a time I had to pull out something to inspire the troops, it was now. If I was out of my depth, the time had come to swim or sink. So, with what remained of my depleted oxygen, I headed for the surface.

Clinically, I dispatched a parent to sit next to the pohwni on the opposite side of the field and keep him in check. I opened my first-aid kit and put two of my parents to work on icing and wrapping the two injured players while informing the subs that, if they ever wanted to prove to me they had what it takes, now would be nice. I grabbed the tearful player like a general in a B-grade war movie and said, *Snap out of it, kid. You are good. I know you are good. And you are dumb to listen to that arsehole. Words are just words. So listen to mine now. You are better than these tears. Go out and show me just how much better.*

Next, I went to the referee and told him I was sorry for the boys' responses to his decisions. We would do everything we could to make sure it didn't happen again in the second half. (I even thanked him for his efforts thus far in a tense, difficult match and also for taking the time to hear me out.) Lastly, in my super-authoritative voice, which has had many fooled for years, I called the boys away from the parents and into a huddle out of the hearing range of parental indignation at sport's unfairness. I directed Mum to compensate for the injustice of it all by handing out Black and Gold jelly snakes to the adults. And, remembering Stephen Smith's warning that angry rants or impassioned speeches had no bearing on the outcome of a match, I resumed a calm, clinical tone and gently spoke to the boys as if I was a big brother counselling them after some girl dumped 'em, *Fellers, if ever you're going to listen to any of the malarkey I spin, make it now. You are losing this game. The opposition is not winning it. If you want to be premiers, play like premiers. For now, you are playing like losers. And that's why you're losing. The referee and the opposition may well be cheating, but I guarantee you, over in their dugout, they feel the same way about us. And you are cheating – you are cheating yourselves. You are letting decisions get to you. You are letting taunts get to you. That's because when things don't go your way, it's easier to sink into self pity than to do something about it. They will be saying the same infuriating things about you even if you were winning this match – even if you won the premiership. Ignore it. Turn the other cheek. Prove to yourselves and to me that you are in control of your tempers, this match and the premiership. To do this you have to get a hold on yourselves and play your natural game. They are – no, were – getting on top of us. And this is the year that we are NOT going to let that happen to us. Boys, do something about it.*

My soccer knowledge is limited – I know that. I could only hope that my intuitive understanding of what made my team tick and the respect that I had for each of them as people not players, would be enough. If I had used up all my evangelical tricks in that glorious match close to a year ago at Radford, then so be it.

But a new team went out on the paddock.

We scored three to win.

After yet another scare, I realised I had to do something about improving the boys' mental strength. Rummaging through my files proved fruitless. But then, while sifting through a little booklet I had prepared for the boys pre-season (which contained contacts, a draw, goals, Huitkerian philosophy, exercises, a picture of Ronaldo and nutritional tips), there in the back section I had placed an article entitled 'General Tips for Mental Toughness Training'. I quite plainly do not read or heed what I distribute. In it, Greg Sargent called for a 'focus on controllables':

> Focus on things within your control. A major source of anxiety in sport is worrying about factors beyond one's control (for example, weather conditions, form of the competitors, winning and losing.) These factors distract you (and your concentration) from the important task at hand – your performance! It is therefore essential to take responsibility for your performances by focusing on yourself, your technique

and your self-talk...and to ensure that all these aspects are focusing on those things which can be controlled. Furthermore, success should be defined in terms of these performance factors and not outcomes (win/loss).

It was as if Mr Sargent had written a personal letter to me. My boys and I were often guilty of spending time during the warm-up sizing up oppositions and discussing their win/loss ratios. We had also got it into our heads that we were a 'dry-weather' side which struggled in slushy conditions (a demon we finally exorcised in the UK). We also often reacted unwisely to referee decisions which went against us – and these decisions were definitely a factor beyond our control, as we had quite clearly learned the previous weekend. Taking a leaf out of Sargent's book, I told the boys that *if* they did enough work to sustain their good form, *if* they continued to enjoy each other and what they were doing, and *if* they worked hard enough to *achieve* pleasing performances, nothing could steal their sense of achievement away from them, premiership or no premiership.

If anything good can be said about consistently winning, it is that it allows you some freedom and space to be creative. At times, I had to fight myself not to restrict the boys' creativity and not to insist that they follow my rigid script of how the game must be played. It is easy for a coach to berate a player for being cocky when at 3–0 up they begin to experiment with turns, back-flips, set pieces and risky passes that were not out of *The Coach's Manual*. This austere, conservative manual will always dictate that you must do all that you can to assure yourself a win (that is, play defensively and protect your lead). But if winning, as Sargent suggests, is the sole outcome a coach, team or club desires, then it can put all too strong a stranglehold on a player's creative development and sense of fun.

Rene Simoes, the brilliant Brazilian coach with the broken English, could be as colourful with his metaphors as he was in his coaching techniques. I was attracted to an analogy he once made between soccer and theatre, my two loves. He said,

> My team has a script. It is like going to the theatre. There are actors there but there is also a script. But at any time the actor can still be himself – he can show his qualities and express himself. That is what I ask my players always. The script is there but you have the freedom to do what you want but not break the harmony of the team.

Simoes was known for instilling 'freedom with discipline' in his Jamaican charges, who all loved to have room to juggle, jink and joke within the rather daunting demands and pressures of having to win soccer consistently at an international level. Or be fired and forgotten.

Matthew was coming into his own in the midfield, controlling it with cohesion and creativity together with Nijie and Jon (who had started to use his basketball skills to hurl the longest throw-ins I've ever seen from a fifteen-year-old); all three were playing the most funky soccer I had seen since they joined up. Jimmy and Cuth were finishing with a panache and derring-do obviously inspired by Big Nuts' distinct lack of self-doubt in front of goal. Blondie was also beginning to express himself as a promising talent with some absolutely sizzling form (which would eventually and finally get him selected in the ACT side later in the year and the Canberra Cosmos Youth Squad some three years later). The reggae was definitely in their souls and I had to be careful not to hog the ghetto-blaster's master switch.

I knew the boys were hip and funky. But was I? With your faithful principal being your side's Number 1 fan and seeking you out every Monday morning in the staffroom to say, *Keep it up now! Don't get complacent!* and with non-sporting colleagues and friends even inquiring, *Can even* you *stuff it up from here?* their genuine concern for my team's welfare had simply become added pressure in my eyes. With coaches from other clubs, divisions and competitions saying, *We've heard a lot about this Radford side,* I found it progressively hard to hear their complimentary tone and only felt the saggy weight of expectation.

We eked out hard-fought victories over the remaining matches and, with every opposition wanting to take a slice out of us, we had to work even harder to secure our unbeaten run in the competition – the Bill Turner and AIS matches excluded. I remember Mark often assuring me that we would win the premiership, but being on the verge of my first real, substantial soccer fairy tale kept bringing out the goblin in me. My reasons were noble: I wanted my lads to have an unforgettable childhood experience; I wanted to exorcise forever the Dutch demon of lucklessness and the curse of a century of failure; I wanted Mum and her sideline of coffee-sipping, biscuit-munching, socialising parents to be momentarily distracted from the delights of their taste buds to see their prides and joys achieve something significant and lasting; and I wanted the good guys to win for once. I wanted it so badly. Sadly, in wanting it so badly, as we got closer to the prize, I started to transform into a bad guy.

I turned into an SSS (sad sideline 'sycopath). Let me explain.

One of the telltale signs that you are turning into an SSS is that you start to follow the play up and down the pitch, using the ball as a magnetic force which buoys you north south north south like a tennis ball in a very long rally.

Another sign is that you don't hear people talking to you. You tend to miss things like *How are you this weekend, George?* or *Doesn't Mark look like he's limping out there* or *Someone's just stolen your car.*

Also, you have an exhausting set of statistics which you can pull out of nowhere. For instance, *C'mon ref! That was the fourth foul Number 7's committed in the last eight and a quarter minutes* or *C'mon boys! We need to score another 2.7 goals to maintain our average of five goals per match* or *Our possession has dropped to 33.3 per cent (recurring) in the last seventeen per cent of the game, in which we only gave a fifty-three per cent effort utilising 43.2 per cent of our brain capacity.* These all eventually degenerate into the ideologically unsound *We have to win three of the last five games to win the premiership so get out there and play like you want it.*

Lastly, you start saying to people things that you really should be saying to yourself, like *Don't let your temper get the better of you! Calm down and start playing your natural game* and *Think about what you're doing, son! You need to get mentally tougher...*and *Why didn't you listen to what I just said to you?*

And perhaps that's the worst trait an SSS exhibits – when he does not listen or pay attention to his players. I would ask kids why they were limping off the field after they had tried to communicate to me that they were carrying injuries during the warm-up. I'd blast them for indiscipline even after they had hinted they had home problems which had been subtly 'dropped' into conversations at training. Too busy being mono-focused, I had ignored the opportunity for important one-on-one moments like answering their e-mails, even if it was only to discuss Pearl Jam's new CD, debate the legacy of Pete Townshend to modern rock'n'roll or having the final say in important philosophical questions like which Spice Girl was the hottest. Or organising Jan Huitkeresque 'sunset sessions' in order to rectify technique. Or unimportant things like helping them with their English essays. Concern beyond the immediate sphere. I should try it sometime.

Unfortunately, when you get to this point, you start to get very self-obsessed and don't even listen to things close to you like your own body clock, friends and, most importantly, your conscience. You have near accidents with stoves, cutlery and cars because you're too preoccupied thinking about the best formation with which to play Majura on the weekend. You can't concentrate at work. One would have thought that I had learned from the *Creative Dribbler* fiasco. My trophy fetish which took root all those years ago had now totally eradicated my ability to put things in any perspective.

But, if you're lucky, these are the times when the

friendly ghosts appear. I remember looking up from the computer one night as I was typing in a match plan, straight into the picture of Dad that rests on the top shelf. His mouth started moving: *You know what your problem is, son?*

No, Dad.

You're trying to win the game for the kids yourself. You believe, a little too much, that you have some bearing on the outcome of things.

You mean, I don't.

You can prepare them in their heads and in their hearts and you do that better than most. But you can't play the game for them.

'Failures at training cannot be compensated for in the dressing room.'

Yup. That's right. Remember what I said to you that time you wanted to quit.

It's up to you.

That's right. And now I'm saying it to you as a coach.

It's up to the boys?

That's it. If they're good enough, they'll win the game. Do you think they're good enough?

I saw flashing in front of my eyes all the manifestations of self-doubt that had presented themselves in my incredible SSS behaviour over the last month: over-preparation, over-conscientiousness and over-stimulation of the cavemanic gland. I'd forgotten that these fellers were more than just chess pieces for shifting.

Yes. They're good enough, Dad.

So what the hell are you getting so worked up about?

We were 3–0 up and it looked secure.

The crunch game had come. If we were to win a deferred Sunday fixture against a gritty Majura outfit, we would win the premiership. That the two remaining games were against two drastically improving and upwardly mobile sides (Belnorth Gold and Weston Creek) was a fact that had not escaped me either. I had hoped to avoid needing to beat either of these improving teams in order to win the crown. If we kept Majura's classy and underrated midfielder in check, then I was confident I could finally be put out of my self-inflicted misery.

With Drew away fulfilling musical commitments, it

gave Lachlan, who had spent a lot of the season waiting in the wings, a chance to play a significant part in the team's aspirations. Although getting minimal field time, he stayed with the side, never complained and never missed a training. Hence, he deserved to be there at the end. He had a normal and expensive adolescent tendency of leaving his clothing and playing equipment merrily dispersed around the many sports grounds of the ACT, so I hoped desperately that he hadn't lost all his gloves now that he finally had a chance to use them.

The boys were confident that it would be their day, after an effortless win twenty-four hours earlier. Mark won the toss and elected to use the strong wind and downward slope at the Dickson fields. I had instilled in him the philosophy of taking a hold of advantages as they were placed in front of him. After all, wind direction, like a scoreline, can change drastically in seconds. So, after scoring three unanswered goals reasonably quickly, it seemed as if we had made the right decision. But in all honesty, if you had asked ol' doubting Thomas before the match how much an advantage the breeze and incline would be under those conditions, he would have said five or six goals.

Using the wind in the second half, that annoying midfielder from Hades gave Lachlan some testing long-range missiles which moved in unpredictable, wind-wavering trajectories through the air and into the back of our net – three times. So, before we had time to register shock, the score was locked at 3–all with half an hour to go. Jono, next to me in crutches, asked if he could go on, but I wasn't all that sure that it'd be the best thing for his knee. I declined, saying the boys would be fine without him.

And for the next twenty-five minutes or so they were fine, wide awake and alert. No longer the wafer-thin wall of defence they had been in 1997, Mark and his troops kept a solid, impenetrable line as the midfielders worked overtime to block any more precarious long-range speculators while distributing counter-offensive balls to the forwards, who were desperately trying to squeeze into openings and find opportunities in the increasingly blustery, challenging conditions. My God, they were looking like a team.

Heroes come from the most unlikely of places. Nijie, who always saved his best for the tough encounters, crept into the forward line from the midfield and found himself on the edge of the box. With the Majura defenders having been obviously instructed to dance the macarena with Big Nuts and hence block off any access to him, a small window of opportunity presented itself to Nij if the ball could be struck by a player with a heart that was both true and blue.

If Nijie was as big and as hopeless a pessimist as I am, he

probably would have got the shakes seconds before impact and glided the ball over the goals. Or worse, he would have completely miskicked it, then spun a somersault before landing with a dull *thwack!* on the sludgy turf of Dickson Ovals (wondering what 'could have been' as his nose sunk deeper into a brown puddle).

In fairy tales, the more modest, unassuming and resolute of characters becomes the most resourceful, reliable and dependable...and always when it counts. In the movies, at the climax, time freezes and everything goes to slow-mo. That's a load of crap. In reality, it happens so fast you nearly miss it.

After close to twenty-five years of waiting for this sequence of precious seconds, a sporting fairy tale finally came true: Nijie's shot sailed into the top netting and even the sight of the Majura 'keeper slowly picking it out of the back of the goals would not convince me it had actually happened. I looked towards the linesman and have never been happier in all my soccer days to see a flag dangling down the arm of a man dressed in black. The goal broke Majura's admirably stubborn resistance and my belief that there was ever such a thing as The Dutch Football Curse.

(I knew Holland would be doomed never to win a soccer World Cup – that is, if all this was really happening and I accepted it as such. But I couldn't help it. I'm selfish,

I guess. I accepted it easily enough, let it stand and robbed the Dutch national side of a finals' spot in both the 1998 World Cup and Euro 2000.)

Speech! Speech!! Speech!!!

(Pause.)

Someone burps. The team laughs, dopily. An embarrassed parent admonishes. Sound peters out. Silence. Then you're up and looking at a huge ring of supporters: grandparents, godparents, brothers, sisters, cousins, next-door neighbours, family friends, doctors, teachers, beaming parents and friendly ghosts – that reassuring supporting cast of thousands who played the essential 'extras' in this movie of ours.

I cannot for the life of me remember what I said that euphoric Sunday. But this is what I would have liked to say: *In time, you possibly will not remember this premiership trophy. They're flimsy things, clumsily made and their arms fall off. But stuck more solidly to your memory will remain a little snapshot of this unforgettable combination of people whom you've shared this incredible journey with. You'll remember them beyond any of the season's wins, draws or losses. And I – er – I will certainly not forget any of you in a great big hurry.*

I looked down at my team – yes, my team – looking

up at me in innocent expectation as most of them had done as green, clueless little seventh graders three years before. After all this time, I realised I'd been wrong not to claim these delightful terriers as mine. I'd loved them as losers and now I had to love them as winners, new an experience as that was for me.

I know it's pathetic, but thanks for letting me know, just for once, what it feels like to win something significant. I wish I could shout you a meal at the Tower Restaurant – like I promised – but you rarely get what you wish for, boys. That's why you should treasure this moment. It's a rare one...

But you know, if I could have just one more wish in the world right here and now, I probably would use it up on having my father here to celebrate this with us. I know how much something like this would have meant to him. To see some rewards for hard work and persistence...

Whatever. Thank you – thanks to all of you – for what you've done...

I remember applause and then lots and lots of people throwing their arms around each other. I remember giving Matthew a hug, once more acknowledging, as we had done all season, that it had all got well and truly out of hand. Then I remember Jenny-May giving me a hug too and whispering quietly in my ear, *I know how much this means to you.*

And that did it. That started the waterworks.

Mum, who had been waiting in the queue of kids, parents and family dentists to speak to me, finally got her chance after the merry commotion, elation and emotion began to gradually dissipate. She held out a packet of some toxic nameless-brand jelly snakes and a thermos filled with Milo and said, *Well done, son.*

She handed me my thermos and didn't need to say any more words. We had that telepathic mother-son interchange thing happening again and I knew she was communicating to me that my earlier wish was an unnecessary one. Hadn't I noticed all this time?

I looked up at the smoky sky, a jaded blue, the colour of crystal Lifesavers.

I had never felt closer to him, since he left us, than I did at that moment. I said, *This one's for you, Dad.*

Dislocation

A siren sky
shed its blood
across the paddock.
And your leg was at a strange angle
when I came with the ice,
one knee where it shouldn't be
bulging
like a cyst.
Hold that on it.

The ambulance
was as slow
as conversation:
*I hope you weren't
going dancing tonight...*
and I told you not to look at it
but you had to
didn't you
once
just long enough to see
that the goalposts had shifted.
It won't be long.

Impact,
cruel and sharp,
had twisted
more than just your knee
off into another
direction.
Keep the ice on it, mate.
Over your face, behind you,
I could see the team
admiring a night sky
serrated by the Brindabellas,
and I found myself
looking blankly
off into it too.

Gemeentelijke Hogere Burger School football team, 1941.
Jan Huitker is the goalkeeper.

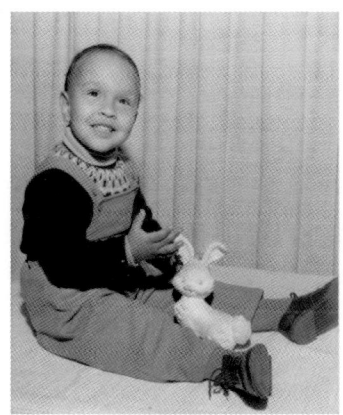

Mum always said
I was a 'rabbit'.
Here I am with my own kind.

The West Woden Juventus Under 8
Division 3 side, 1975.
That's Zelco back row, third from left.
Sean the goalhog is pretending to be
an Air Force One pilot.

The Marist Minor Cup winners, 1977.

*Even when sick, Jan Huitker
could see the funny side of things.*

*Preparing to march
in the Kiss Army, 1979.*

After her heart attack in 1997,
Mum's Sideline Café enlisted some helpers.

Radford's first Division One Premiership-winning team
– the under 15s 1998.

Cuth gives the ball a hoof with Matthew and Coach Huitker watching.

Goalie Drew.

Captain Mark.

Hero Nijie.

Long-legged Jimmy.

Blondie, Fattie, Frenchie and Keysie.

Exploring London, January 2000.

Taking in The Breadknife in the serene Warrumbungles, Central NSW, far away from the soccer fields on our post-season hike, September 2000.

The 'visiting team' at Old Trafford, 2000.

Warming up before a typically soggy English fixture against Lymm High School, Cheshire.

The bench at Woodbridge, Suffolk, looks on, spirits inflated by proceedings.

Scenes from HMT's stage production of Not Just Footy (June 2004) featuring Jake Fraser as little George and myself as my father.

3. Extra Time: Not Just Footy

The inside might be black as the night, but at the end
of the tunnel there's a light.
– Andrew Lloyd Webber, *The New Starlight Express*,
2000

Since I began playing soccer, every coach I've ever
come across has at some point said the same thing to
me: football is about more than just kicking a pigskin.
Or, these days, kicking synthetics.

From his vantage point post-side, Dad would continually
push me to look for patterns of action occurring on the
other side of the field, particularly those which allowed
for a rapid switch of direction and possession, which
would in turn allow the defence to open up and give
an opposition attacker a one on one with yours truly in
goals. What happens off the ball, he might have said,
is sometimes just as important as what happens on it.
The judicious coach would go further to add that what
happens off the field, at training and in the backyard,
is also as important as what happens on it.

However, the time had now come to move into a larger

backyard, to not only move 'off the field', but right off the map. The last thing I felt necessary to provide these boys, as my father had done many times when I was young, was a trip into the magical world of 'overseas'. So it came about that, for the first time in my life, football was literally taking me places. And I vowed that around those eight tour matches where focus would well and truly be on the football, a lot of happy, hungry and hard-earned living and learning would most certainly have to occur away from it.

Just this once, I was going to worry a little more about organising the itinerary than compiling team lists or scribbling match plans. Much as I wanted to learn about British football technique, I knew I would be just as hungry to see and hear about the places and people outside of stadiums where real living actually occurred.

As for the boys, at least initially they seemed willing to be led once more into the unknown. I knew that, regardless of what happened on the football pitch and any minor traumas, trials and tribulations associated with travel, this would be an experience they would never forget. Where time might erase scorelines and even oppositions from the memory, it finds it harder to remove significant places.

And significant people.

It is a daunting adventure in itself to take sixteen adolescent males overseas on a sporting tour. It's not the sort of thing you'd find a lot of volunteers for. You hear horror stories of tours going hopelessly wrong, with team members being left behind, kidnapped or executed in hostile, foreign countries after straying from the group.

I had visions of our more vague team members missing flights after taking absent-minded one-way strolls into the desert from Dubai International while foolishly looking for a doughnut stand. Or having one of the team's resident loudmouths incarcerated by some intolerant, humourless customs official for making a joke about bringing his pet Uzi along for the flight.

So it was with some apprehension that I boarded that Emirates flight for Heathrow with my Radford First XI soccer side and intrepid team manager Bruce for what was to be a three-week journey into the heart of The Country Which Lives and Breathes Football.

Bruce is a living saint and I don't say that just because of his religious sensibilities. He is a man incredibly generous with his heart, time and knowledge. He has a general knowledge second to none, which would make him a killjoy at most quiz nights; there are not many men his age who could hold their own in a conversation with a teenager about The Verve's breakthrough release; a sports fanatic about the most potent bowling combinations of Sussex County Cricket Club (1836 to the present day); a thespian on the better shows at the West End (including where to get cheap tickets); and an old, sentimental, floral-frocked, voluntary tour guide on famous one-legged Bulgarian choristers working in eighteenth-century England. A meticulous researcher, organiser and manager, he made the perfect foil for his more whimsical, arty, somewhat careless coaching companion.

Bruce, God love him, had all the facts and figures of every school, team and place we were going to; when, where and how we were going to get there, with approximate arrival times; the likely scoreline between our teams; as well as more arcane things such as Emirates' safety record or how many pairs of thermal undies and socks would suffice on average per child per week for the trip's duration. And where best to pack them.

Packed with enough thermal gear (thanks, mums), deflated soccer balls and a team kit heavy enough to send the plane plunging into the Indian Ocean, I was surprised when our collective baggage weighed in under our official weight allowance upon leaving Canberra. That would not be the case on the return leg.

Arriving at Melbourne, we found the entire female Emirates staff dressed in flowing Arabian scarves attached to an intriguing rectangular shoebox on their heads. It was there and then we realised one of the fringe benefits of team travel. Your noisy, excited, adolescent group gets immediately ushered into the next available check-in booth, where an Emirates staff member instantaneously transmogrifies to check your side in. This is while a long queue of crusty-faced small-time customers who have been waiting for hours silently festers behind you. To add insult to injury, our check-in chick was a young, voluptuous, amiable lass, although I found it quite hard to take my eyes off the shoebox on her head.

We had heard good things about Emirates – even the refresher towels and dunny paper reminded us that they were Airline of the Year 1999 – but special praise must be reserved for the nifty personalised video screens which helped pass the hours cramped like a proverbial sardine in economy class. I believe Emirates allows some precious centimetres of extra legroom, a bonus not lost on my predominantly long-legged footballers like Jono and Jimmy. Unfortunately, except for a *Black Adder* episode about Samuel Johnson's dictionary and a short Australian film called *Fetch*, we had to wade through a total of twenty-four hours of unmitigated tiny-televised crap for the duration of the trip. Just like TV at home!

Along the way, the boys relieved tension by attempting to order beers, battle Economy Class Syndrome by playing a soccer-cricket hybrid with a shoe in Singapore International at some ghastly early hour of the morning, and nearly getting executed in Dubai when Keysie had trouble comprehending the mumbled Arabic directions of a sordid, sworded airport security guard who obviously thought 'hacky' was what you did to recalcitrant tourists as opposed to fuzzy little balls full of foam beans.

In flight, Bruce put a ban on the dubious drink ordering, which worked really well as prohibition until, two hours out of Dubai, I tried to order some red wine for myself. I evidently have retained some youthfulness – despite having coached this side for five years – and was bluntly refused alcohol by the hostess. She glared at me with a look evidently reserved for crushing delinquent little boys then marched off in a big huff to serve someone with a more serious, adult request. I had to let my herbal Noctogen tablets and the gentle Gulf turbulence rock me slowly to sleep. Damn that woman, I thought, every time Ozzie pushed me half-dazed off his shoulder.

At least I didn't have to wear a ridiculous shoebox on my head.

Gulliver's Sports Travel had arranged eight fixtures

which would see us play both state and private school teams from as far south as stony-beached Brighton to the sodden, northern plains of Manchester, while taking in the sights, sounds, smells and surrounds of the counties within which we found ourselves. From London, we were to be equipped with our own coach (that is, bus) and a foul-mouthed, philosophical, entrepreneurial and highly skilled (try reverse-parking a bus in London or negotiating the Reebok Stadium car park) Mancunian driver, a 'character' in the true sense of the word, by the name of Teddy, whose personality, opinions and profanities would become indelibly imprinted on our psyches.

We had four days to kill in London and finding things to do there was hardly difficult. On the way into the city from Heathrow Airport, we passed one recognisable London landmark after the other and I remember turning to Matthew and saying, *This is really getting out of hand now.* I could see his mouth force out a knowing smile as he continued taking in the very real sights of his first overseas country. *You can say that again, H.*

No sooner had we thrown our suitcases onto our hotel beds than we had to get out and paint the town red. (Someone had obviously already started on the buses.) I was as excited as the lads. I still had to pinch myself in order to believe that coaching soccer had finally, in fact, got me overseas. I sent my Dad a small, spiritual prayer of thanks for introducing me to the marvellous sport of soccer, instantly forgetting the heartaches (both mine and Mum's) it had caused and those desperate days descending into the Holman Street lagoon to retrieve a thousand soggy soccer balls.

We decided to go out for a walk, soak some gamma and find our bearings. I figured this would be the best thing to do to defeat jet lag, despite the fact that our excitement levels had totally eliminated even the mere idea of a snooze from our bodies. I was keen to start at Trafalgar Square, which I had visited twenty-two years earlier with my parents. All I had wanted to do was feed the pigeons. There was nothing more blissful to me as an eleven-year-old. I thought I was Mary Poppins. *Feed the birds, tuppence a bag.* Eleven-year-olds are rarely hard up for entertainment.

So it was, at Trafalgar Square, a pigeon found its bearings. Right on young Harold's clean jacket. Our team 'baby' and latest inclusion couldn't have been better initiated into the rigours of being in a touring side. Being a close-knit group, we all naturally pretended it hadn't happened and I can assure Harry's parents that absolutely nothing more was mentioned with regard to pigeons, Trafalgar Square or his bespattered jacket for the remainder of the tour. You may be intrigued to know that Churchill's Statue at the Houses of Parliament has an electronic censor near Winston's cranium which acts as a kind of force field as it niftily zaps away the unsuspecting pigeon 'pre-poop', so to speak, just like an elaborate mosquito lantern. We had Harold fitted with one straight away.

The next morning, a tour bus took us for a whirlwind tour of London. With the exceedingly knowledgeable Suzanne as our tour guide, we were taken to all the major points of interest. Suzanne was a bit kinky when it came to William Wallace and we all found it a little unusual to start our tour of this grand city by visiting his memorial stone outside St Bartholomew's (where they filmed scenes for *Shakespeare in Love*). But who were we to argue? Or care? We politely took photos of ourselves sporting sexy Braveheart poses underneath the plaque. Suzanne looked on lasciviously, purring.

We also took pictures of ourselves draped over things like the big stone lions at Trafalgar Square, and took delicately shaped team snaps in front of significant British institutions such as Big Ben and the Houses of Parliament, Tower Bridge, Kensington Palace, St Paul's, Buckingham Palace, Harrod's and, last but not least, Donuts & Company, Piccadilly Circus. From the bus we took in the Old Bailey, the Tower of London, The London Dungeons, The Globe, a busted over-hyped ferris wheel eyesore called The London Eye, the HMS

Belfast, Leicester Square, Albert Hall, Westminster Abbey, the 10 Downing Street front gates (which a loony attempted to drive through about a week later), The Ritz, Marble Arch, and Green, St James' and Hyde Parks. The remaining three days were then left for us to sightsee London at our leisure, the details of which I will return to shortly.

With a McHappy Meal at McDonald's being far too expensive, at almost £3, for even the most hardened fast-food junkie, Donuts & Company became a financially and gastronomically attractive, zero-nutritional value substitute, so popular among teenagers of today. The boys also found their appetites dragging them into local Tescos where, for about two quid, most could leave with a 19p bread roll, an assortment of meats and spreads, fruits, a chocolate bar and a can of drink. Far better value than a pattie of mad cow.

But while in the centre of London, home-based at the geographically superior Regent Palace Hotel, we had to urgently find a cheap place to eat together at nights that would happily hold sixteen famished adolescents. Despite the boys' pleas, I suggested that they needed some variety in their diet, having already spent a fortune on small, round cake goods with gaping big holes in the centre. *There's heaps of variety, H*, one team member debated with me. *You can get chocolate, strawberry, boysenberry, caramel, banana...*

Our first night's meal wasn't too bad: a deep pan buffet for £5. But the trouble with touring adolescent boys and the 'All You Can Eat' concept is that all they see on the sign is 'All the *Pizza* You Can Eat', leaving the wholesome salad bar untouched and glistening in the far corner. And if you think you'll so much as see a slice of any Meat Lovers left to get cold at the nether regions of the pizza bar, then you'd seriously have to think again.

Our prayers were answered by the busy little West End Kitchen in Panton Street. 'Good food at great value!' said the business card. A cranky, overworked sourpuss waitress took us down a flight of stairs and put us in what was probably once a dungeon for torturing those who didn't pay for their meals. There, the boys would usually load up on pasta dishes but I would always take a set menu three-courser, provided it had some sort of dessert soaked in custard. This is a habit, dear reader, one pays for in full somewhere down the line.

The food came faster than you could imagine it being cooked. Our plates were cleared within seconds of slurping in the last noodle of seafood fettucine. As mastication and conversation are things not imperative at the teenage male's dinner table, this place proved ideal.

And, on the topic of cuisine and bad habits, it was apparent throughout the tour that most Brits commenced the day with a Full English Breakfast. We all religiously started the day with an exciting FEB at the Regent Palace. My boys were not ashamed to ask for seconds, obviously used to generous portions at home. They were, in response, given a rather Dickensian look of incredulity and disgust by the parlour maid, who would then unceremoniously thrust another sausage and hash brown onto the empty plate with total and utter disdain and a spooky, brooding silence. Her maidly motto for life was obviously *Mustn't grumble*. As the boys returned for thirds, a stiff upper lip was maintained as my growing lads systematically cleared the pantry each morning. I could imagine her stocktaking each lunchtime, smashing her fists on the kitchen table and weeping profusely. Poor thing. We were possibly the last Australian schoolboys team allowed to dine at the Palace.

An FEB includes every possible item of fatty food guaranteed to send you in for an angioplasty by the end of your holiday. Every English person I meet insists that the FEB concept is just a 'thing for tourists' and they in fact eat quite healthy breakfasts, thank you very much. Then they'd waddle off, cantankerously, fat butt cheeks squeaking.

The worst in the 'cantankerous' category would have to be London shop owners. Have you ever met a more cranky, menopausal lot than the London proprietors of restaurants, music outlets, museums, coffee shoppes, ticketing booths, hotel lobbies and bird-feed stands? With the exception of the punt operators on the Cam, I have never met a bunch of people more morbid about their lot in life than these crusty plodders, plonkers and trouts (to use Teddy's terminology). It was as if the cold weather had permanently frozen a constipated frown on their faces. Surely the performance of the English cricket team wasn't that depressing of late?

The schoolteacher in me would always insist that this tour was a cleverly disguised chance to give these kids a rich educative out-of-classroom experience. Using soccer as a fulcrum, I was going to increase single-handedly their life vocabulary with a range of new people, places and traditions that would make them more wholesome men of the new millennium. Don't laugh; we teachers love framing objectives in grand, magnificent teacher-speak. Achieving them's another matter.

I had made it clear to the lads at the outset that our trip would be a sporting, social, cultural and historical experience, recognising that I would have to work particularly hard on the final two. To the average teenager, the very words 'culture' and 'history' conjure up respective connotations of nerds gazing lovingly into Petri dishes and overweight textbooks crammed with lots of irrelevant dates.

So I decided to kick things off by whetting their appetite for things cultural and historical, albeit footbally, by visiting the overpriced and overrated FA Football Hall of Fame on the Thames – fully stocked with the English penchant for crappy wax dummies, some of which were meant to resemble vaguely the likes of Beckham, Bergkamp, Cantona and Zola. To me, the glowing, rustic smiles on their faces made them look more like a motley collection of Scandinavian goatherds dressed in footy gear and ready for a mighty frolic on the mountain with the goats. The boys, with less developed imaginations than mine, just found them tacky and became quickly uninterested. And judging by the speed in which they paraded through the FA Hall of Fame, and later the Manchester United Museum at Old Trafford, I figured it best to avoid museum excursions, even sporting ones. So much for my objectives.

(Later, outside the famous Bat and Ball Pub at Hambledon, the 'cradle of cricket', the shoulders shrugged and apathy reigned. And this was the place where English cricket had its first headquarters and the rules of the modern game were formulated. This was also, quite evidently, another boring sports museum disguised as an interesting drinking establishment. Oh well, there's no pleasing some. Mind you, the English cricket team would give most people reason to drink.)

Cricket enthusiasts in our touring party were finally

coaxed by Bruce to partake in a tour of Lord's (where they were curiously mistaken for Japanese tourists) while I took the philistine remainder to the bohemian Camden markets, where some economic learning occurred. Jono got himself a three-week tattoo from some washed-out Camden hippie, which came off in the shower the next morning. (If, perchance, that washed-out hippie has picked up this book second-hand at some Camden literary gypsy's bargain stall, I must tell you that Jono is going to return one day to get his money back. You have been warned.) Jono then proudly showed me a cigarette-shaped lighter – the butt section flicked open to reveal a natty little flame – which he purchased for his sister *for only a pound!* There were obviously bargains aplenty at seedy Camden.

Concerned that I was the only person in Camden who didn't look like a member of The Cure, I escaped to the tube station at Mornington Crescent only to find it was closed. For reparations, of all things. I commenced my walk to the nearby Kentish Town, desperate to get out of bohemia and go somewhere different, like Soho. But when I got there, I was accosted by a million Robert Smith clones desperate to sell me a second-hand CD. So I decided to go back to the hotel and plan a training session.

After three days of sightseeing, I felt the time had definitely come for the boys to kick a cowpat around. Despite the attractions and distractions, the lads were keen to get a ball at their feet. I lost count of the times they were kicked out of the hotel lobby for playing hacky. We hopped onto a moving, pulsing red, double-decker bus heading for Hyde Park and promptly ran up to the top level, where you can have a right royal perve at what life on first floors around London is like first thing in the morning.

At Hyde Park we got changed on the bandstand and then, after a warm-up jog around the lake and through the woods, we found a relatively flat portion of turf and went through some skills and drills. People passing by took photos, possibly thinking we were significant in some way, and an Arabic chap, Abdul, joined us for a scratch match. I had no idea that he was a pensive soccer intellect: *Sorreee. You boyz dey hev – how you say – goowd skeeel. Yes. Goowd skeeel. But – very sorreee – dey hev not goowd – how you say – runningk eento owpen spazzes.*

I thanked Abdul and invited him to show me where the 'spazzes' were, as I thought he might have been referring to my midfielders. He dragged himself off, fifteen minutes later, having touched the ball three times, looking like he'd just been doing sprints training in the Sahara. *Dare, you seee. Tooo mutch owpen spazzes.*

I thanked him again and invited him to our opening match in Bulgaria.

I would be telling an awfully big fib if I didn't admit occasionally to steering the tour to places I wanted it to go – much like the boys' on-field play. Like a parent, I came endowed with the tragic delusion that I had a far greater idea about what was to be fulfilling, beneficial and of long-lasting interest to an adolescent than the adolescent himself. So, like a parent, I was in for a rocky time of it.

Being a drama teacher in my other life, I was keen to hit the West End (for attractions other than cheap meals) and journey into the magical, musical, colourful subway that is *Starlight Express* at the Apollo Victoria Theatre. I bought half a dozen tickets in the half-price booth, thinking they'd be easy to resell to the boys. What a once-in-a-lifetime experience!

Unfortunately, when a teenage mind is made up about something, like *Musicals suck big time*, you'd sooner convince a lion to become vegetarian. Now I'll admit there's something a little odd about singin' and dancin' ultraviolet trains on roller skates, but I had to resort to sheer, unadulterated guilt and belligerence to sell the remaining tickets.

Fellers – you'd love it. It's a once-in-a-lifetime opportunity to see a musical here. There's singin' and dancin' trains and – and – what more could you want? Buy the bloody tickets will you, or I'll be so shitty. And put you on the bench for the first game.

With one ticket left, I did what any desperate man would do: bully the youngest. Harold bought my last ticket. After checking that his jacket was now cleared of the last bits of residue from aerial spatter, six of us headed off to the Apollo that evening and had a night to remember.

An incredibly huge-budget multilevel set, elaborate and glowing costumes and make-up, and some annoyingly catchy show tunes made it a far superior night than loading carbohydrates and slurping caffeine at Donuts & Company. We were treated to mind-bogglingly flowing, lyrical poetic genius such as *We carry weight/ 'Cos we are Freight/And Freight/Is great.* Wow. Andrew Motion must be aware that his days as Poet Laureate are numbered. But in the end, it doesn't matter, does it? Inanity can be quite uplifting in the musical context. At least those six starry-eyed lads who went with me can proudly put on their CVs that they saw an Andrew Lloyd Webber at the West End.

Hearing Harold happily squawk *There's a Light at the End of the Tunnel* at spontaneous moments throughout the remainder of the tour certainly made it all worthwhile for me. I think this also became Bruce's theme song towards the tour's conclusion.

As I've hinted already, I'm a devoted Beatles fan. And the last time I had been to England I missed out on doing Fab Four-related things. I was determined not to let that happen a second time. Recently, Beatle George had nearly joined John in the great hereafter after yet another deranged loony decided a Fab Four member's time was up. It must be a blessed nuisance being unfortunately famous and always having people wanting to do maligning things to you and your loved ones. Dave Beckham and Victoria Adams, the most talked-about couple in Britain at the time due to 'the underpant-swapping caper', would have to keep baby Brooklyn Spice – who I assume wears her own nappies – on a very tight leash. She would have to be Number 1 on some pathetic baby-napper's most eligible toddler list in England. After all, as Salman Rushdie said about the world of popular music, which I would extend quite happily to the sphere of football,

> ...the fans as well as the artistes – sometimes seemed to be populated exclusively by people with troubled minds.

So, without further ado, I took my troubled mind and sixteen impressionable young ones off to St John's Wood to hold up the traffic at a zebra crossing on Abbey

Road. One driver in a Lotus told us, *Give it op, you sad basstids,* as he waited for Bruce to finish his impromptu photo shoot from a nearby traffic island. I guess there is something pathetic about a man my age walking across the road in bare feet in the middle of winter BUT THESE THINGS MUST BE DONE. I'm a real, devoted fan. Anyway, anyone who actually drives a Lotus must be a sad basstid in the first place.

Naturally, it didn't look at all like the album. The cover of *Abbey Road* must have been taken from the middle of the road, where you are in obvious danger from un-nostalgic and cranky Lotus drivers. So the angle would always be wrong. The light was bad (*Here comes the sun!* said one bright spark) and the trees – so bushy and big on the original picture – seemed bare and hardly formidable. And there wasn't a little white Volkswagen with a 28IF licence plate to be seen for miles. We did get the chance to be of help to some fellow tourists. We kindly assisted, encouraged and photographed two cautious yet somewhat voluptuous American girls on the famous zebra crossing. But they were big chickens and wouldn't take their shoes or any other clothes off. Or join us for the rest of the tour.

We returned to the city with me feeling a tad uncertain as to whether I had wasted the boys' time. Then, a few days later, I noticed during one dull bus trip to somewhere in England, Keysie – the cheeky sod – had brought my copy of *Sgt Pepper's Lonely Hearts Club Band* with him. He was singing *With a Little Help from My Friends* gazing serenely into his colleague's face, obviously not thinking of a Dubai Airport Security Guard. I found this all strangely apt. I considered it a minor triumph that one of my team was listening to something a little more musically substantial than gangster rap. You can hardly sing *The Nigga Ya Love To Hate* to a pal in the bus.

I had failed in all my attempts to see Agatha Christie's *The Mousetrap* at St Martin's Theatre, London's longest-running show, clocking up an impressive forty-eight years. So Bruce, worried that the nagging thespian inside had not been satisfactorily sated, plotted a late-night raid on The Globe.

There had been an aborted attempt to visit The Globe, the most singularly inaccessible sight to see in London, earlier that day. I don't know what possessed Bruce to attempt this slightly unwise late evening peramble. It was close to midnight when we finally got to the theatre, without the aid of the Tube – and that was after walking through back alleys and side streets in which I was sure we would be blissfully murdered by a Ripper copycat. In any case, I touched the building, Bruce took some flash photography and I tried helplessly to recite some

Hamlet. The boys with us, realising this was a reasonably significant moment, respectfully waited for me to show off a little and talk nostalgically to an invisible skull in my hand. But in my deliriously tired, unmurdered state, I could find nothing but Andrew Lloyd Webber's train songs cheerfully asserting themselves through the fog in my head.

So, instead, I recited,

> *We never sulk*
> *We hulk the bulk*
> *Cos Freight*
> *Is great!*

On arrival in England, it was surprising how complimentary everyone was about Australian sport, especially in the afterglow of the netball, cricket, rugby and tennis successes on the world stage. I would have assumed that our Aussie sports heroes would be loathed to the very core of their talented antipodean bones. With the English national sides struggling in most of those codes at the time of our arrival, I was a little nervous that perhaps the British might be overestimating my little school side from the nation's capital, assuming in turn that I had brought a coach full of Harry Kewells with me on tour.

Oh well. The trip is, after all is said and done, about learning things. If we were to get overestimated then ruthlessly thrashed, at least we'd learn something about our chosen sport along the way. What doesn't kill you makes you stronger, right? There's the ever-optimistic coach talking.

I have some theories as to why English sport is regressing to the dark ages, and would like to present a few modest suggestions to rectify matters. Stopping the Full English Breakfasts would be a start. Then, accessibility to decent training fields would certainly help. Every pitch in England is muddy, uneven, tilted and looks as if it's been pillaged by a mob of rabid badgers or landed upon by aliens. Why anyone would want to train seriously on them is anybody's guess. On top of all this, it is pretty dark by four p.m., so unless trainings are factored into the school timetable – as they were at Rugby School – you would normally finish a session of stretching as the street lights would come on and stars would shoot. Improved indoor facilities – and more of 'em. That's what they need, in a nutshell. Not that anyone cares what I think.

In any case, at least initially, it seemed the unofficial-in-fact-not-previously-known soccer 'ashes' would be well and truly returning to Australia. By the halfway point on the tour, we were still undefeated, with easy wins at Brighton, Warminster, Woodbridge and Ely, amassing over twenty goals, conceding only three. Each of these locales had schools which served as a central geographical point and, being in the middle of their respective locales, I found it amazing that students wandering around the campuses were never collected by drivers suffering from a bad case of road rage so evident on the windy, village roads across Britain. *Sorry I'm home late, dear. Had to hose a couple of kiddies off the bumper.*

Each of these schools also had very distinct playing fields. It became an interesting match statistic that the first twenty minutes of every game would be scoreless as we became used to the idiosyncrasies of the various surfaces and the English sides which, aided by benevolent referees, quite literally threw everything at us, such as particularly late slide, open-studded and sandwich tackles. Connecting with the ball appeared not to be of paramount importance. The oppositions were, despite all this, very polite and would frequently apologise to the Radford boys they had come close to hospitalising – reeling in agony and prostrate there on the ground before them.

Brighton's picturesque pitches were three miles from the school, nestled in a valley through which an icy sea breeze swept across a lopsided field. The Brighton captain directed us to the pitch while quite insensitively (and, in retrospect, unwisely) apologising to me for how dull and dreary he thought our home town Canberra was. Being multiskilled, he had toured there with a rugby side a year ago. As I looked to my left and right, I tried to figure exactly where he was coming from. Unfortunately, Teddy heard him and, sensing my discomfort at hearing my home town so unreasonably denigrated, chipped in, *Listen, y'Brighton lads are gonna get yer arses whipp'd – y'kno that? If I were ewe, I'd be crappin me bloddy punts a-boat now. These Ossies are pretty ruethliss fuutball players. Yop. I'd be gettin ready for a right-roy'l whippin. They did not travel all this way to play tiddlywinks, if y'kno wot I mean, lad. Better ewe than me, son. Tha's fer shore.*

Needless to say, he had never seen us play. I wanted to kill him. Bruce blushed like a tomato. The Brighton lad gulped nervously.

Despite a barrage of unpenalised fouls, the Radfordians were never seriously challenged and won the game 7–1. A vindicated Teddy hunted for unwary Brighton students to gloat at: *I toll ewe sew!*

(Later, we were generously given a numbered W.S. Blackshaw print of an oil painting of the front gateway, as well as a school tie and accompanying pin – and then told never to come back. They had evidently forgotten that their rugby side nearly scored a century at Radford a year earlier. So na na dee na na.)

With the boys off with their billets, Bruce and I were keen to explore Brighton. This was the town where, in February 1963, Jan – sorry, *John* – Huitker first received a letter from the sexy, athletic, new boarder whom he had been chatting up at his mother's house in The Hague. He was returning to Australia (after Uncle Theo's recent remarriage in The Netherlands) and spending time with Theo and his wife trying to work out the attraction of sitting on bum-numbing stones by the Brighton seaside watching a limp surf crawling in. I imagine he got lots of buttock indentations smoothed out by kicking up his heels and humming happily along the pretty piers when that letter arrived from sexy, athletic Jeane.

Bruce and I were especially cautious, as everyone had warned us that the place was notorious for roving, raving, rabid homosexuals. This made Bruce, dear family man from Gungahlin that he is, ultra-paranoid. *Look over there, George,* he'd say, two *men!* As we walked the Brighton streets looking for a decent feed, Bruce continually pointed at any all-male configurations of two and quietly, under his breath, whispered to me, *There's two more!* This all came to a halt when I asked him what exactly we both looked like wandering longingly together through the deserted Brighton streets with hungry faces.

I've always had a weakness for penny arcades, so visits to the tacky, fluoro carnival piers of Brighton (and later at Blackpool) to sink a few hard-earned pounds into the graphics wonderland of soccer video games were greeted warmly by me. (I still go on the very unscary Haunted House rides at the Canberra Show and enjoy the living ghoulies out of it.)

The next morning we celebrated Simon's birthday at the Palace Pier, Brighton. There, the boys exhibited a masterful skill on these infernal machines nurtured by spending days in front of their respective computers and Nintendos at home when they should have been juggling a ball out in the garden. Or doing their homework.

I became sadly addicted to an amazing £1 soccer game. You insert your gold coin and then kick a real soccer ball into a backing board below a huge screen. Then, somehow, the vital stats of your kicks – such as its trajectory, velocity and the brain capacity of the kicker – are digitally transferred to the screen, where a computer-generated goalie, electronic crowd and digital scoreboard adjust themselves according to how well you strike the kick. I wish I had had this gizmo when the boys were in Under 13s and it was a rainy training day. It sure keeps the kiddies entertained for hours. In truth, the boys absolutely caned me, despite my spending about £10 trying to improve at it in order to beat someone. I even challenged Bruce to a game. I doubt I would have beaten a legless man. Those machines are stupid anyway.

The remainder of the Brighton trip was spent spending. The boys, totally undermining the stereotype that all girls wanna do is shop till they drop, began their ritual search for doughnuts, clothes and souvenirs. Perhaps the biggest bargain on tour was a 50p rubber chicken which, for reasons I initially could not fathom, Blondie purchased at a One Pound Shop. It followed that, whenever anyone on the tour was cantankerous for whatever reason, he would be systematically pummelled by the chicken until he discovered a more mirthful temperament. This is, ironically, quite a difficult thing to do while being bashed over the head by artificial poultry. But there you have it.

Perhaps the majority of London's shopkeepers could in fact use a damn good whacking across the head with our chicken in order to improve their collective mood disorders and general stuffiness.

Just a suggestion.

At a myriad of places, Blondie's chicken, that symbolic sponge of foul humour, would be suddenly photographed: in the hands of saints in a multitude of cathedrals, outside Buckingham Palace, puttin' on the Ritz, eating at the West End Kitchen, atop Blackpool Tower and wishing it was a duck, Merseyside.

I would like to digress a little here.

These shenanigans may sound a tad familiar to you. It is all very much our little take on that garden gnome caper, you know, when 'gnome-nappers' would steal from some unsuspecting person's garden their chief gnomic figurine, only then to take it overseas, where they'd photograph the little fellow beaming outside exotic locations such as the Eiffel Tower, the Taj Mahal or the Statue of Liberty – wherever the thieves were going for their holiday. The 'thieves' would then send back to the distraught owners photographs, letters and postcards from the 'napped gnome in question. And this could go on for months, years.

I read recently that these gnome-lifters are evidently growing in stature and had formed the Garden Gnomes Liberation Front, which saw fit to liberate twenty from the Parc de Bagatelle, where some two thousand smiling statues had gathered to, well, stand around for some reason. A member of the GGLF claimed responsibility in the press and it was big news, reported nationwide. I kid you not.

I write this as a cautionary tale for Blondie. But also to remind people in an analogous manner how easy it is for silly things, like kicking a pigskin around a paddock, to become bigger, more ludicrous and out of control than they really need be...

Stonehenge, which we visited en route to Warminster, held some mystical attraction despite being nestled between two motorways on the windiest of Wiltshire plains. And despite being equipped with the English Heritage's penchant for user-friendly cordless info-phones which had, crammed somewhere inside it, in every language including Swahili, every possible recorded historical fact, figure and anecdote about the site in question. Walking through Stonehenge, you would have thought you'd landed in the middle of Yuppieshire, UK, tourists everywhere holding little black phones to their ears and nodding pensively.

As I write, a mob of forty volunteer loonies is apparently about to recreate the huge journey made by the original builders of Stonehenge, and intend to carry a three-tonne lump of bluestone from the Preseli Mountains in Wales, from some nifty-sounding Welsh place mellifluously named Mynachlogddu, across the Bristol Channel, then up one of the Wiltshire motorways to rock mecca central. The volunteers will travel close to four hundred kilometres, travelling at five kilometres a day.

I wonder how much like geese they'd all collectively feel if some Agent Moulderesque sort of myth-debunker suddenly proved that the rocks were actually teleported by aliens. These discerning little green men with almond-shaped heads so pitied the primitive state of prehistoric earth that they provided the apes, who would successfully evolve to be the soccer hooligans of the future, a celestial sundial as an act of alien good will. Of course, if they had landed inside a London shop in January 2000, they probably would've just dumped the rocks on the proprietor's head and then left.

The White Horse near Westbury, a huge chalk hill carving allegedly cut to commemorate Alfred's victory at the Battle of Ethandunein against the Danes in 878, was similarly awe-inspiring. The cameras clicked hungrily; I guess a horse carved into a hill is not something my team had seen every day of the week. In America, they carve ex-Presidents into mountains; in Wiltshire, they're inclined to subjects more equestrian. I learned that the strange but goodly folk of Wiltshire have in fact a total of nine white horses niftily etched into downs about the county, the one in Westbury being the oldest. Finally bored with horses, some chalk-horse cutters, termed leucippotomists (yes, seriously, someone gave them a name) moved on to pandas, kiwis and, I kid you not, a map of Australia (on a regimental badge). Go to Salisbury if you doubt me. You gotta love a creatively restless leucippotomist.

At Warminster, we were placed on the small, school pitch, complete with a crumbling brick wall surrounding it, an oak tree one metre from the corner flag, some rather severe undulations (upon which no one had thankfully carved a horse) which created some intriguing dips and bends across the boggy paddock – all overlooked by the stern facade of the St Boniface boarding barracks, an intimi-dating building near the northern goals. Remembering how my boys coped with the undulations at Illaroo Farm, Nowra, all those years ago, I was reasonably confident that they would manage here.

What followed was another barrage of unpenalised fouls, rapid apologies, more fouls and an eventual easy 5–1 win. Despite the results, the Warminsterians seemed keener for us to return: our tour captain, Blondie, was asked if he would consider the 'Gap' program at Warminster (and perhaps coach their firsts while boarding) and a group of female cheerleaders who thought our lads 'lush', 'cute' and 'not bad' were also keen to know how long we were boarding at the school. I was later informed that a team member had successfully 'swapped saliva' at Warminster. And for the next two weeks I had to mail Jono's underarm deodorant-scented love letters to somewhere in Wiltshire. (His new nickname, incidentally, became 'Lush'.)

Teddy had got us all very excited when he informed us that the next town visited on tour was where Jane Eyre used to live *and happily writ all those girlie books of 'ers. And when she'd finished with her cookin' and cleanin', she'd go out on these streets and no doubt have a jolly delightful peramble.* Hang on a minute. Did he say Jane *Eyre*? This excited my nerdy, literary self. (I couldn't wait to get to Stratford-upon-Avon to see the laneways and bridges where King Lear, Macbeth and Falstaff used to play ball games and then moon the passing carriages.)

The lads were quite gobsmacked, to use an English phrase, by the Roman Baths, situated in Bath of all places, before which I gave a little lecture on the evils of donuts and shopping malls. It went a little like this: *Boys, if you think Bruce and I are going to let you spend every waking hour visiting the shopping malls and doughnut shops of every historically and culturally significant town we come across on tour, then you have got it quite wrong. Pay attention to this, please. Your parents have forked out close to four grand for this little sojourn. This may surprise you, but this trip is actually about a little more than just a sporting jaunt in England where we blissfully kick a pig skin around all the pretty schools on our itinerary. You will now walk, with smiles on your faces, into that Roman Bath, pay Peggy at the booth whatever the admission price may be, and get educated and cultured – even if it kills me.*

A nearby touring group of elderly Americans gave me a round of applause. I felt like John F. Kennedy.

We consequently spent a reverent and surprisingly pleasant hour equipped with 'info-phones', wandering through the catacombs, aqueducts, viaducts and thermal pools within this masterpiece of Roman ingenuity. Here, underneath the city, existed the remains of a culture some two thousand years old, through which one could still wander and touch and feel the ambience. This is something hard to do in Australia. And it all felt *real*. Unlike pictures in a history book, it unfolded and rotated around you like an IMAX in overdrive. I remember feeling the same way about experiencing my first Premier League soccer game, realising it wasn't all just an image on a TV set, but almost like some huge, living, teeming fairground, with myriads of people, stalls and attractions spinning around you at a hundred miles per hour.

From there, we got some fresh air sauntering along the grand, sculptured Georgian streets and bridges (such as Pulteney) in one of England's most grand and elegant cities, through which the River Avon cheerfully flowed. British townships can sometimes really get that picturesque thing happening one hundred per cent correctly. Some boys thanked me for taking them there. Some vowed to return. Now that, from a teenager, is not small praise. Bath was a hit. And some were getting hungry.

We cleaned out the Bath Soup & Pastry shop, making the owner's profit charts hit an all-time high. With display stalls emptied to the crumb, she immediately went to the travel agency next door and booked a ticket for herself and a bag full of ingredients to Australia.

Soccer history and culture was difficult to circumvent. A dinner at Hunter's Moon, a pub owned by former FA Cup winner and Chelsea defensive axe Ron 'Chopper' Harris, found us happily digesting its owner's footballing anecdotes as well as a charming roast and Yorkshire pud followed by a dessert deliciously drowned in custard. Mrs Harris even appeared, to give me some cooking tips and accept a little genuine adulation for food preparation skills. Chopper then disappeared into his house, returning minutes later with moths flying out of his head and his FA Cup Winner's Medal (won in a replay 2–1 against Leeds in 1970) and the European Cup Winners' Cup Medal that followed (won the following year also in a replay against Real Madrid, 2–1 in Athens). Chopper's teams obviously liked winning games 2–1.

I told him his medals were very impressive and that I understood the symbolic importance of trophies to the fragile male psyche. He suggested I have a beer.

Then followed a refreshing discussion about the state of football and I was happy to hear his terse denouncing of the greedy, soulless, money-hungry nature of the modern game. I would have shouted him a beer but for the fact that he owned the pub.

167

I don't know how Chopper went over with the boys. They no doubt recognised his achievements as being significant and boys are always partial to people with a hard-arse reputation. I remember wishing I had some footage of Chopper in action to show them before our visit to Hunter's Moon. It was not, after all, until I saw Gordon Banks' save against Pele that I truly recognised him as one of the great goalkeepers. And Chopper Harris belonged to a black and white mythology pretty far removed from Roy Keane in technicolour. But I guess that's the adolescent thing, isn't it? They have to be left to discover the significance of the past in their own time. For now, sadly, Snoop Doggy Dogg beats the living piss out of old-fart muzak like The Beatles.

The playing fields at Woodbridge were a groundkeeper's pride and joy, billiard-table smooth and manicured with love – only a tad muddy underfoot. To be fair, soccer was possibly not the school's pride, joy and primary concern. They scrambled to get a makeshift team together of rugby players and even an Australian 'Gap' exchangee. (Pre-Kewell, to use an Australian in your soccer team was the definition of extreme desperation.) After the ritually slow period of commencement, where the fouls reached a new plateau of polite, unassuming violence, the Radfordians kept a level head and politely returned fire with the quite novel weaponry of soccer skill, handing back an 8–1 drubbing. I was given the school prospectus.

That night, at my Woodbridge billets, I was pleasantly getting my ears chewed off by my host's son, who was very keen on some book which, at the time, seemed a lot of nonsense to me. The story centred on this young wizard called Harry Potter, who went to some magical institution called Hogwarts. My ears pricked up when young Adam told me that they played a game at the school called Quidditch, which involved four balls, two of which projected themselves *at* you and were intriguingly called Bludgers, a playing ball called a Quaffle and a rogue, bonus ball called a Golden Snitch – and, yes, I am sure I heard correctly. The players, divided into 'Keepers (God bless their cotton socks), Chasers, Beaters (every team has them!) and Seekers, utilised an array of broomsticks, clubs, goalposts and magic chants to achieve their objective, which like any sport was evidently to win lots of games while endeavouring to humiliate the opposition teams.

There was a lot going on here. I asked Adam what would happen if the Bludgers were lazy and simply wouldn't budge? And what if a Beater accidentally whacked the Golden Snitch? That'd be catastrophic. I'd assume then that the Chasers and Seekers would go and have a right royal philosophical Quaffle. And the 'Keeper, dejected, would take his goalposts and go home.

Adam snorted and replied, *You are really very impertinent,*

George. I'm going to bed.

I said, *Na na dee na na, Adam.*

This Quidditch, Hogwarts and Harry Potter hoo-ha: it'll never catch on.

I think I have deep within me a castle fetish. I can truly understand why wacky people hire them out for nuptials. So, when Teddy suggested that we storm Leeds Castle at Maidstone prior to the West Ham / Aston Villa game in London, I seized the opportunity. As you enter, you walk through an impressive wood garden full of attention-seeking peacocks and a duckery full of, well, ducks. I prophetically named one Peggy.

Unfortunately, aside from the beautiful grounds, the actual castle was packed with evil old 'explainers', a demonic crew of volunteer historians ready to devour the attention of any unsuspecting tourists who should catch their gaze or walk in their trajectory. We did get some significant exercise wandering through the wood gardens and running away from explainers.

Nearly every town we visited had an outstanding cathedral, abbey or architectural structure of some sort and I remember vividly a spectacular crimson sunset over the impressive Ely Cathedral, its formidable octagonal tower tastefully floodlit in the dwindling light of early afternoon. With Benedictine foundations that were close to a thousand years old beneath our feet, as with the Roman Baths, the boys became increasingly deferential to the history that surrounded them, almost awe-struck. But not Harry. When told the actual cathedral section took one hundred years to construct, he turned to me and asked, *Why would you bother?*

Our tour guide, a lovable duck who I think was called Peggy, waddled us through the numerous sections of the cathedral and introduced us to the Ely Cathedral ghost. Ooooo. I love spooky things. She thankfully didn't see our chicken hanging limply from a statued saint's outstretched, sublimating arms.

The football pitch at Ely was again miles from the school and apparently below sea level. The marshy earth must have affected the goalposts because they looked sunk, about a metre short of usual height. There was a plaque near the fields dedicated to a Humphry Smith Esq.:

A Man who in every Station of Life Acquitted Himself with Honour, Integrity and an Upright Mind, Of a Competent Knowledge in the most Useful Arts and Sciences, but most Eminent for his Superior Abilities in Draining Fenny and Marsh Lands.

Fair dinkum.

Despite Humphry's grand legacy, the Radford team's flowing game became a little like playing water polo in peanut butter and we were nearly officiated out of the game by a referee described by one of the Woodbridge parents as 'ye olde Adolf Hitler'. Nonetheless, our Radford Aryans, led by Blondie, notched up the fourth win, knocking four between the Lilliputian goalposts.

The next morning, we were all up bright and early for a church service.

Bruce had volunteered the services of a player for the readings. I was nervous as most of the boys' literary palette did not venture further than a Snoop Doggy Dogg *Doggystyle* CD lyrics booklet. *I think you'd better do it, Bruce.* The reading was 'The Good Samaritan', extolling the virtues of selflessness, tolerance and philanthropy. I figured the boys would be better served listening to it.

It was great seeing my team at church. Surrounded by a thousand years of religious architecture, tradition and fervour, it was mighty difficult not to feel in some way spiritually humbled. I was lost in contemplations profound and pure when I was tapped on the shoulder by a voluptuous young English teacher who then commented on how gentlemanly the boys were, particularly for a rugby team. (Why is it when it comes to sporting events all the pretty girls never know what's going on?) In any case, I stammered out some inanities about koalas, while secretly both envying and loathing the Ely lads for getting the chance to study *Paradise Regained* under such fantastic conditions. I was about to ask her how I was to go about enrolling in Milton 101 when the organ struck its first wavery chords and she gave me a glistening smile and said, *I hope they sing up nice and loud.*

Up to this point, with the exception of the chicken's occasional appearance in the arms of Ely's saintly statues, the boys and Teddy had been well behaved. I had fears of Teddy walking in and saying, *Nice fockin church y'have 'ere.* But I had been spared any embarrassment thus far. The boys were lifting their hymn books quite angelically and I believe I saw the sudden and inexplicable appearance of a halo over crew-cut Cuth. However, I had grave fears for their singing.

I would like to digress here.

What is it with boys and singing? Why is it always so difficult to get males to sing anything except neanderthalic football chants or dirty pub birthday songs? And why do male singers always try their best to sound terrible when they do warble? Why is the concept of melody and harmony so difficult for us to master?

Male rock singers like Bob Dylan, Peter Garrett and those cantankerous punks have a lot to answer for. Lots of attitude, sharp lyrics and – hey – great tunes. It's just that none of this lot sees any need to actually *sing* any actual notes. Then there's the Bee Gees, who should be shot for making the whole concept of males hitting (very high) notes together notoriously poofy and silly. And as for rap, which dispenses totally with melody and harmony and focuses its cranky energy on raging tunelessly against the machine, I'm really at a loss. Most rappers need a good thwacking with the chicken. Oh boy, I'm showing my age.

I remember as a kid happily chirping *Redback on the Toilet Seat*, *A Windmill in Old Amsterdam*, *Tip-toe through the Tulips*, *The Elephant Song* and a host of ABBA ditties while jumping on and off my bed. At parties, I'd always come equipped with my ukulele and lyric sheets. I mean, this pulls in the chicks. I worked that out at ten. While all the other guys are trying to impress each other by smoking in the bushes and wearing pretend earrings and fake leather, I'd try to impress the girls with my lovely, authentic voice. I tell you, a singing male is a rare and desperately treasured thing. Go on, ask the girls if you doubt me!

As Aunty Willy will testify, when her niece had her eleventh birthday party, she was asked who she wanted to invite. She burbled out a list of seventy girlfriends and then added, *I want George there too.* I brought my ukulele, song book and even learned some Kamahl love songs, like *A Daisy a Day*!

And here we were, in January 2000, about to impress a voluptuous young governess and her petite, elegantly skirted charges in the romantic cloister of Ely. It was a daydream, right out of D.H. Lawrence.

The boys' choral lead-up work to date had included shouting *The Drugs Don't Work* in a variety of unrelated key signatures, as well as a charmless but loud rendition of *Daydream Believer*, a favourite of Teddy's, in which the concepts of melody and pitch were entirely abandoned. But I knew I could count on Gatley. Girls love him. He'd made an art form of being goofily lovable (except on the soccer pitch, when he turned into Edmundo the Animal). Undeterred by the stares of basically everyone around him, the annoying restrictions of key and time signatures, or the fact that he did not know the hymn at all, he belted out with absolute zest and fervour a sentimental but raucous bush interpretation of *O Praise Ye the Lord* – Number 65 in the hymn book – which had the congrega-tion running, reeling and rolling in the aisles. God love him. (We never saw the teacher or her girls again.)

We left our mark at Ely Cathedral. At least Bruce did. Still wearing the boots from yesterday's swampy game, up he went and read his lesson about the Good Samaritan. It was just as well we were all concentrating on his mellifluous voice as, below, finely sculptured hoof prints of Humphry Smith's fenny and marshland mud were being deposited on the white altar carpet, trailing all the way back to Bruce's seat. He then spent the rest of the service praying fervently that nobody would notice his abominable staining, much as I did as a teenager. God looks after her own. (He got away with it.)

God must have heard Gatley's angelic strains and immediately reciprocated by greeting us with an angelically sunny day as we exited the cathedral. We decided to spend it at stodgy ol' Cambridge, a day which will live long in the memory. I encouraged Gatley to try and audition for the King's College Choir.

Bruce had nagged at me all year to take the boys punting on the River Cam, which I had initially pooh-poohed. (Incidentally, A.A. Milne's original facsimile of the Winnie the Pooh series is apparently nestled in the nearby Wren Library archives, along with the sexy Mr Milton's *Lycidas*.) Across from The Wren, Nevile Court, adorned with delightful cloisters, was apparent-ly where Newton first calculated the speed of sound. He wouldn't have been allowed to calculate and ponder on the grass if he was still alive today.

The smell of the Cam, coupled with a fear for my

players' collected coordination levels, made punting a prospect akin to being trapped in a historic Leed's Castle Chamber Room with a ninety-year-old 'explainer' dying to give his uninterrupted two-hour spiel on Henry XVIII's little known fondness for sculptured dog collars. In other words, it was best avoided.

My fears were unfounded. There would be no danger of my lads breaking the sound barrier with their clumsy punting. After arguing the price with the punt-hire operator from hell, the boys enjoyed a fine hour viewing Cambridge's architectural splendours from the comfort of their punts. Sadly, I was nearly shot, arrested and then hung in the Great Court for taking photographs from the manicured grassed area Cam-side by a university security guard who actually looked a lot like Richard III and who needed a good dose of the rubber chicken. As I have hinted, every patch of Cambridge grass is littered with an abrasive, butt-ugly *Keep off the Grass* sign. I bet Salman Rushdie, of whom we are about to hear more, kicked a few down in his time there.

Stratford-upon-Avon, however, is perhaps not the best place to take a bunch of footballers. And the Thatch Restaurant with a pricey, fine (that is, quality not quantity) three-course meal next to Anne Hathaway's Cottage, was perhaps not the wisest place for a bunch of footballers to lunch. (*Does Anne still live there, H?*) Tesco, after all, would do the job more cheaply.

Similarly, visiting Shakespeare's burial place at the Holy Trinity Church for 50p was far better value than paying ten times that to see the quaint, restored cottage that once belonged to his Uncle's Best Friend Wilbur, who ran the local pub and whose sister, Gertrude, had a unique and uncanny gift for croquet.

In the Holy Trinity Gift Shop, I encouraged the boys to buy hardcover copies of Shakespearian sonnets for their girlfriends, being the thoughtful guy I am. The proprietor could not believe the business I generated on hardcover sonnets (*Should I get her a hardcore copy, H?*) and I was suddenly, in the gift shop, blessed with a beautiful vision of a harem of Canberra girls smiling serenely in the sunshine as they were compared to a summer's day by their reformed, enlightened, footy-booted boyfriends recently back from the UK. *Er, that'll be £3.50, thank you, sir.* Oh yes, sorry. I was daydreaming.

Stratford-upon-Avon is full of bookshops where you can buy classy, relevant literature such as *The Complete Illustrated Shakespeare Volumes One, Two and Three* or, as Lachlan discovered, the *Unofficial Spice Girls Sticker Book.* I bought the latter without hesitation, the best two pounds spent abroad.

Warwick Castle was a far snazzier fortress than Leeds Castle – that was the boys' verdict. It provided the opportunity to victimise the younger members of the team in the torture chambers (complete with the customary Madame Tussaud's wax dummies), but sadly the armoury room was closed so we couldn't play in the nifty iron suits. We could, however, scale the dizzy heights of the ghostly turrets with exceptionally eye-catching views of the Warwickshire countryside. Sigh. It was another view hard to leave...

I was leaning against a turret watching dusk starting to fire up on the horizon, thinking how sweeping heights can create their own brand of melancholy if you let them. And how it would be great if Dad was maybe as close as Utrecht now, a sea away, less than an hour by plane, on some study trip to his old horticultural haunts and uni days. The beautiful, spooky, sculptured gardens below would have spoken to him in their own planty way. Then a voice from behind: *You OK, H?*

Yeah. I'm just enjoying the sunset. You?

Yeah, I'm fine.

Not homesick or anything?

No. Well. No. A bit. Miss me girlfriend. This castle's pretty sick.

What did you like the best?

The torture chambers. They were mad. What about you?

This view. I like things that remind you about how big the world is.

Yeah. It's pretty spec. (Pause.) You know, I reckon I'll come back here.

Really?

Yeah. This trip's been awesome. England's been awesome.

In what way?

I dunno. Bit like what you said. You know, like the world's bigger than you ever thought it was and stuff.

Who would you take?

My girlfriend.

To the torture chamber?

Na. I'd save that for my little brother. (Pause.) He's a little turd. (Pause.) You know, the things we've done, these places and stuff – and the games and shit – I reckon me ol' man would have had the maddest time here.

I think my Dad would've had the maddest time here too.

Yeah.

You reckon we're gonna win tomorrow?

Sure thing, if you put me on.

We'll see.

You reckon a photo of that sunset'll come out?

Na. It's never as good as the real thing. But you'll need something to remember it by. So give it a try. If the photo's crap, you'll always remember how good it really was in the picture you keep in your head...

He took out his trusty instamatic, aimed and fired. Then gave me a salute and left.

I stayed a little longer, tracing a winding river through hamlets and townships and snaking off into a hole in the horizon, allowing a moment's brief, sentimental wallow. I really hoped that boy's photograph had caught something of this alluring view. And then I hoped that his whole damn roll contained a monumental sequence of snapshots from a time he'd find difficult to erase from the memory.

You can see it, can't you? A nostalgic man, who probably doesn't play soccer any more, occasionally returning to that old school sports album over a soothing cocoa.

Especially when the world feels a little cramped and stifling and little things like memories and photographs sometimes help to open things up again.

That's a pleasing picture.

You'll never get a game there, I was told by our travel agent. *They get asked to play fixtures all the time.*

Yes, but that's of rugby. I want to play them at soccer.

I couldn't tell him that it greatly appealed to my perverse, if not slightly disturbed, sense of humour to play a game of soccer against Rugby School. Besides, I bet no one prior to me had thought to ask them for a fixture other than Rugby Union.

He said he'd try to arrange it. And my gamble paid off.

Rugby was similarly an impressive school to visit and was a popular tourist destination during the recent World Cup of Rugby for some reason. We were shown around by a kindly librarian named Rusty, a sort of a Warwickshirean Harry Butler, who had a sound working knowledge of the significance of every geographical and geological corner of the college and every person – past or present – of any note.

Incidentally, should any of you wish to send your child to board at Rugby, it is a mere £5,460 per term. It's a sound investment. And I'm sure your son will thank you for the rest of his life – you know the way kids do.

Unless his name is Salman Rushdie.

I believe this former petulant Rugby student was not entirely complimentary about his time there. I picked up his general feeling for English boarding schools while reading his new novel *The Ground Beneath Her Feet*:

> Cyrus Cama was sent away to boarding school..., banished to an implacable hill station establishment which based its methods upon the tried and true British principles of cold baths, bad food, regular beatings and high-quality academic instruction, and which helped him to develop into the full-blooded psychopath he afterwards became.

Of course, Rusty was quick to point out to us that their famous student body included the likes of Matthew Arnold, Rupert Brooke, Lewis Carroll and Thomas Hughes as well as (dramatic pause and sigh)...a certain Mr Rushdie. I was itching to ask more about young Salman, but Rusty had one of those librarian looks which said something like 'Mr Rushdie would have got a little more out of Rugby had Mr Rushdie given a little more to it'. So I left it alone. (I was also dying to ask him if he had read Rupert Brooke's poems *Lust* or *Thoughts on the Shape of the Human Body* but decided to let sleeping dogs lie.)

It is without a doubt that Rugby's most famous son was William Webb Ellis, a maverick student from the class of 1823, who decided to 'pick up the ball and run'. Rusty stopped us beside a plaque by the William Webb Ellis Field, which he reverently read to us:

> This Stone Commemorates the Exploit of William Webb Ellis Who With a Fine Disregard for the Rules of Football as Played In His Time First Took The Ball in His Arms and Ran With It Thus Originating the Distinctive Feature of The Rugby Game. AD 1823.

I might have rewritten it as follows:

> This Stone Commemorates a Fat Bully by Name of William Webb Ellis Who Had No Friends and Like a Typical Petulant Loner Decided to Wreck a Perfectly Jolly Game of Soccer By Taking The Ball In His Arms and Challenging All The Smaller, Puny Junior School Pipsqueaks to Wrestle It From Him Thus Originating A Distinctive Stereotypical Feature of Most Boorish Rugby Exponents For Centuries to Come. AD 1823.

Just joking!

After visiting the outstanding school museum which chronicled the school's history from 1567 to the present day and featured biographical data on literally everything but Salman Rushdie, it was quite apparent that Rugby deserved a lot more than just a cursory glance from the sporting (or literary) enthusiast. But, if you weren't still rugbied out, you could peramble through the James Gilbert Rugby Football Museum in town.

On the morning before the fixture, we were treated to yet another chapel service. Knowing that my boys only pray if losing, I was not certain how they'd cope with another religious service after Ely. It all opened with yet another hymn, possibly *O Praise Ye The Lord for Young Webb Ellis* or *The Lord Is My Scrum-Half*, then a brief dramatic reading by some costumed students. Then the young pastor stood up for his sermon and said, *Lord, for the gift of miracles we are truly thankful. Amen.* Everyone replied Amen. Then within five seconds the chapel was empty. It was the fastest church service I'd ever sat through. That the sermon went for one sentence was to me a miracle in itself.

We had a good game against their Under 16 side. We were refereed by a real dandy gent who, in my imagination, had, prior to the game, replaced his pipe with a whistle, patted the corgis and made his way to Rugby on his trusty penny-farthing: *Jolly nice bunch of lads, George. They played hard and fair. Deserved their win. Credit to you ol' chap. Nice skills, what! Anyway – must dash back to feed the corgis, get the kettle on, so forth...*

185

Despite losing 3–0, they appeared grateful to be playing visitors in a code other than rugby. And did not place a fatwa on any of our heads.

We were now smack bang in the middle of a busy sequence of fixtures. As we headed further north, our moment of truth finally came on the sports field with close losses against stronger sides at Oundle and Lymm Schools and an unlucky draw at North Cestrian Grammar. Each of these schools had players 'on the books' of a number of football league clubs (such as Crewe Alexandra, Stockport County and Port Vale). Oundle, who had travelled to Australia for the 1998 Kanga Cup in Canberra and won in both their age groups in tough competitions, were no strangers to international tour matches. The Lymm side, sporting an Argentine World Cup strip and a similarly flamboyant style of play, had recently returned from a successful Spanish tour. They were not soccer lightweights by any stretch of the imagination.

I'm not going to degenerate back to being a pathetic, one-eyed, immature, excuse-giving wanna-be coach who is living far too vicariously through his players. I just kinda wanna say that maybe – just possibly – at Oundle and North Cestrian the intricacies of the offside rule have yet to be explained to anyone. And hey, it's obviously standard practice for their coaches to referee tour games. That's cool. That's groovy.

(Just kidding, right!)

Oundle was nothing short of hospitable. Their coach, a cheerful chap we affectionately named Mad Max, took Bruce and me for a very pricey meal at an elegant pub called the Falcon Inn in Fotheringhay, where the ghost of Mary Queen of Scots – she was executed in a tower nearby – overlooked us munching on pigeon.

On the field, the Oundletics in fact chased like rabid homing pigeons (sorry to continue to use this simile so insensitively, Harold), frustrating our possession-based game into submission, making scoring immensely difficult. Their captain, a pleasant, elongated fellow from the Cayman Islands, was very humble and complimentary: *We invent the game, and you Australians show us how to play it.* They gave us an Oundle crest, book and school tie as well. That made them a hell of a lot easier to lose to.

After the unlucky loss at Oundle, Lymm was obviously a class above us. That made them a lot easier to lose to as well. Two of our goals came from a bizarre sequence of uncoordinated-goalkeeping errors. Possessed by some fumbling demon from Hades, the Lymm 'keeper had two inexplicable spasms of stupidity while collecting loose balls and, on one occasion, quite strangely threw the ball into his own net and then, minutes later, presented our advancing centre forward, Cuth, with a simple tap in from one metre. The 5–3 score line flattered us somewhat, despite Jimmy's clever consolation goal after some neat lead-up work.

On the other hand, North Cestrian was a dour, pedestrian but well drilled outfit having a centre forward with severe delusions of grandeur, paranoia and a possible twist of unresolved childhood trauma. They drew the game 1–1, late in the match when their striker was so far offside that he was waiting for the ball in Bulgaria. After consulting with an invisible linesman, their coach/referee did them all a favour and blew the goal. We were flummoxed, but it was far too late in the tour for us to get cantankerous about it. We, of course, are above all that. We did, however, leave mud all over their change room, shower block, toilets, sinks and mirrors. Na na dee na na.

I cannot explain how exciting attending an FA Cup or Premier League fixture is to the uninitiated. Whether you are a soccer fan or not, it can be a spiritually uplifting moment. Laurie Daley wrote in his recent autobiography *Almost a Winner*,

> You could have a crowd of 600 over there, but they'd make enough noise to make you believe there were

20,000. I have often felt like taking a Bruce Stadium crowd over to England to show them what it's like. It would be fantastic if we could generate the same kind of atmosphere in our matches back in Australia.

I could empathise with Lozza. I remember going to Raiders and Brumbies games upon returning from the UK and wanting to jump on my chair and single-handedly – and God knows I probably could have been heard over their woeful cheering – admonish the Bruce Stadium faithful for being so limp.

We had been treated to an FA Cup tie and two Premier League fixtures along the way, which found us soaking up the electric atmospheres of grounds such as Highbury, Upton Park and Anfield. The English may not be winning much on the international sports scene, but could we ever come close to matching the passion of their fans at these sorts of games?

Teddy had an uncanny ability to park the tour bus right at the front gates of any stadium he took us to. He seemed to know every policeman on a first-name basis and then would often say rude things about a) their wives, b) their sexuality, c) their looks or d) all of the above, generally when they were a few seconds out of hearing range. He also was pretty good at driving while standing up. He'd frequently do this when facing in the opposite direction to things like his windscreen or approaching traffic and often while telling us a complicated joke which would require facial expressions and exuberant gesticulation. (In these instances, he'd steer with his knees.) In retrospect, that he actually got us to the stadium alive was quite an achievement.

Approaching Upton Park, the boys and I received our first real glimpse of football fanaticism as Teddy ducked and weaved the 'boos' through a million cars (each sporting a little West Ham United shirt with 'Di Canio' emblazoned above the number 10) and swarms of maroon-clad supporters evidently with more important things on their minds than avoiding getting squashed by a big boos full of Australian schoolboys.

When the game finally got under way, we were suddenly sprinkled with what appeared to be light rain. Sadly, we were to discover that it was actually a minor sunshower of saliva, a very unfortunate side-product produced alongside some pretty frothy abuse by a herd of pohwnis behind us. They were, in turn, showering disdain upon *their own players*. In truth, at no point during the whole Upton Park match did I ever get the impression that the home fans actually liked or supported the home team West Ham. It all seemed like a big hassle, such as the prospect of a proctological examination, to be encouraging these miserable, overpaid plonkers in the middle (to quote an astute analyst behind me).

So when Paulo Wanchope – the poor old Costa Rican 'plonker' with a penchant for finishing the immensely difficult but totally botching up the plainly simple – missed an open goal from less than a metre, it was just as well we were all wearing our trusty maroon rain jackets. Firstly, they did save us from a second angry tidal wave of assorted, soaring mouth fluids. And secondly, as the opposition Aston Villa was predominantly maroon as well (their home strip is, in any case) – a colour that both of these teams obviously stole from Radford College Soccer Club strip – everybody around us assumed we were either a youth squad from West Ham or visiting Aston Villa. As fans of both clubs evidently felt that no young player would ever have a shining future at any of these clubs, we were treated with supreme apathy. As the match progressed, it became increasingly difficult for the boys and me not only to ascertain who was supporting whom, but who was playing whom and for what rhyme, reason or result. So, intoxicatingly exciting as the cranky, foul-mouthed atmosphere was at Upton Park, it was hard to feel anything but blissfully neutral, like the players in the centre who obviously felt pretty neutral about the whole match as well. It ended up 1–1. Go, maroon.

Yet being present as the Liverpool faithful, led by those standing on The Kop, resoundingly sang *You'll Never Walk Alone* (albeit before a drab 0–0 draw against Middlesbrough in which Michael Owen painfully walked off alone and injured after ten minutes) made me slightly embarrassed about the half-hearted manner in which we sometimes mumble our national anthem in schoolyards, sports fields and services. The boys were again quite gobsmacked at the intensity of the chanting, cheering and abuse hurled from the stands. I was inspired to write a poem.

The boys tried to attract the attention of Middlesbrough's dynamic Australian goalkeeper, Mark Schwarzer (a hero in the tense Socceroos World Cup qualifier penalty shoot-out against Canada in 1993 – a moment when I certainly did radiate an inner glow). He was quite a preoccupied fellow during his warm-up routine, but found time to say *Hello there, lads* after a voluminous rendition of 'Aussie Aussie Aussie Oi Oi Oi' attracted his attention while reeling in high crosses. In subsequent games, Schwarzer fumbled crosses and shots and let in pathetic goals because of a voodoo curse I put on him for not paying my boys enough attention. Sucko, Mark.

As we were in Liverpool, I quite shamelessly indulged the boys in a nostalgic Merseyside mystery tour through *The Beatles Story* at Albert Dock, where the boys got to buy Fab Four memorabilia for their ex-hippie parents (such as Sgt Pepper mouse mats and Yellow Submarine fridge magnets) while I wandered shamelessly through the excellent exhibits humming *Penny Lane* and chanting *All You Need Is Love*.

In Manchester, we also spent an unforgettable day at Old Trafford, on an organised tour which took us into the actual stadium, where we relished the opportunity to sit in the stands, dressing rooms and dugouts. Blondie could not resist sitting where, after confirmation with the ultra-keen tour guide, Ryan Giggs' royal Welsh arse would be found in the sauna-equipped home dressing room on match days. (The visiting sides, naturally, don't get the warm tub.) Me? I pretended to be Gordon Strachan in the visitors' box, on a rare day that Coventry City would defeat the reigning champions away from home. The team then savoured the chance to run down the players' tunnel towards the hallowed turf – something many of us had only dreamed about doing at some point in our lives – and get some sort of notion of what that might feel like...

Even with the stadium empty, the ghosts of a 60,000-plus capacity crowd still make a lot of noise.

Then later, in the Oxnoble Pub in Manchester (getting tickets for a 'Reds' fixture against Arsenal being as difficult as finding a cheerful Londoner), a kindly publican let our boys in to watch this traditional grudge match on the big screen. As the Guinness flowed around us, the boys witnessed first-hand the zeal of Manchester United fans as they swore, cheered, pleaded and prayed their way through a tense 1–1 struggle with the Gunners (yes, another draw) as if their very lives depended on the events unfolding miles away.

One particularly vociferous, foul-mouthed fan with impressive biceps and a ponytail (who introduced himself to me as George) and who obviously would marry the Manchester captain Roy Keane at a moment's notice, said to me, *Mate, I can't stand that faggot Australian goalkeeper. That nancy should go back to where he came from with all his faggot Australian friends.*

I saw no reason to disagree.

Despite being winter, we did not experience a day of rain. The thermals – alas, mums – were never unpacked.

As the sun, which shone down on us when it shouldn't have for three weeks, descended somewhere over the northern tip of Norway, this magical little mystery sporting tour finally came to an end.

I had been too excited to read books on the flight from Sydney to Heathrow. So, loaded with Robbie Slater and Frank Farina's biographies and *Staying Up*, an account of Coventry City Football Club's 1997/98 season by Rick Gekoski – which Bruce spotted for me in London (I obviously wasn't totally soccered out just yet) – Teddy rolled us into Manchester International Airport. His farewell speech was heartfelt and poignant: *Well, get the fock off me coach and get back to Aussie, you feral tossers.*

No point in gettin' awl sentimental and shite. One load of tourists off, next bunch of plonkers on.

Emotionally moved by his words, we left him our mega-sized Australian flag for his grandson, a Radford umbrella for the non-existent rain and, like every other day on tour, a coach littered with cans, chocolate wrappers, plastic bags and half of Lachlan's clothing.

Yet, as I was wheeling away a trolley of luggage, I turned back and saw him ruffling young Harry's hair one final time while throwing numerous items of goalie apparel at Lachlan, and swearing at the top of his voice. I remembered feeling that maybe Teddy had said just one time too many that he wouldn't miss us when we go and that England'd be a better country when we *sodded off back to all the feral wallabies and wombats.* And took our blowflies with us. He pulled his 'boos' away, with the Australian flag still hanging forlornly in the window.

It's hard not to get close to people you travel with. Especially when the journey is a good one.

Anticipation about getting home nullified the potency of Noctogen for most of the return leg, although the Emirates in-flight viewing could be relied upon to send one into a brief burst of catatonic sleeping pleasure. And I figured there was no way I'd get served any wine.

Wanting to prolong the feeling of travel, the boys bought duty-free Snickers bars, orange-flavoured Clinique cologne and bizarre Arabic patisserie (a doughnut substitute, no doubt) in Dubai. We put a bag over Keysie's head so that the security guards would not get the urge to decapitate it. And Lush kept us on our toes by leaving his passport on the plane.

In Melbourne, waiting seven hours for the connecting flight home, it was hard for Bruce and me to believe that we were back on our home turf, to overuse the footballing metaphor. It did give me some invaluable time to think after a two-hour shower.

I knew it wouldn't be until a little later that we would all truly recognise what a wonderful way it is to receive an educative introduction to a country while keeping yourself fit and active in the process. After all, our English school counterparts had participated in similar sporting tours to places such as Spain, Cyprus, Barbados and Australia. I really believe these lucky lucky kids are all the richer for it.

We returned with five wins, two losses and a draw; a cohesive, improved and hardened band of footballers; and a catalogue of unforgettable places perhaps to return to one day. It was, for me, hard to believe that this would be the quintessential chapter of a book I started writing about twenty-five years earlier at a pristine little Curtin paddock when I hit the earth with that dull *thwack!*

I don't know if seeing the West End lights had got me thinking about theatre again, but for a long time after returning from the UK I kept seeing soccer in theatrical terms. Academy-award winning director of *American Beauty*, Sam Mendes, once likened theatre to sport:

> You can go into a rehearsal room and you can chuck a ball around and you catch it or you drop it and you can see where everyone else is... You're part of the team.

I quite like this sentiment. Sport, at its best, is wonderful if it allows you to interact, learn from, evolve and create with an energetic, focused group of people. If any of these four things are absent, that's when the chinks appear in the armour.

In theatre, art constantly mirrors living. There on the sports fields, you can also readily liken sport to life. The game at times can feel so *real*, so much like the characters in a moving, lifelike play. But there's the rub. It isn't life. It's just a game. An elaborate form of theatre where significant meaning is necessarily metaphoric, fabricated.

Trainings are just like rehearsals, where the players, in

both instances, are asked to create circumstances, then 'chuck a ball around' in order to rehearse *being in* these circumstances. So when the 'season' commences they can approach a new and public circumstance with some preparation, confidence and familiarity. Although there are many variables, they should, if all goes smoothly, perform towards their optimum level when it really counts. If they have trained effectively, a win or a winning performance will sometimes ensue.

And while, like a good play, a good game can provide understanding and allegorical truths that you can take with you back into your own life, it is not, fundamentally, any more significant than that.

As I've hinted before, real significant life happens somewhere else: in family kitchens, small suburban ovals, cancer wards, angioplasty units, in love, in quality time, on buses, on the way to work. In many ways, this little trip to the UK provided an escape from all of these 'realer' life experiences. Yet, for all its fantastical elements, it also provided learning, fraternity and a real human experience – all those things about which I had begun to whine that sport was no longer capable of providing. Up until then, my dissatisfaction with sport was something I had left relatively unexamined. An excellent article by Norman Abjorensen, 'Looking for a Place Within', later recon-firmed some of my feelings that sport and I had reached some sort of crossroads:

There is a sublime of transcendence in travel that, if not experienced, is surely akin to living the unexamined life. As many writers have found, to travel and to seek new experiences and knowledge is far more than a geographical journey; travel can tell us as much about ourselves as we learn from the changing world about us. It has been long apparent to me that when we travel we are in a curiously heightened mode of perception, all of our senses stretched and extended to rake in as much as we can of new things about us.

It was clear to me that the boys had certainly had their senses stretched through sport and travel. A new world of possibilities was opening up for them. Mission accomplished. But, as curtains began to be pulled open for them, I was curiously being dragged in the other direction. Could it be that maybe this was as good a time as any to let the curtain fall on my sporting journey?

I had decided as a new year's wish that I had to force a closure on some things: life had become so convoluted that it was getting harder to enjoy richly and thoroughly the many things I do. As an actor/director, I had long since made a vow that I would never do a production 'for the sake of it'. I would only accept a role or produce a show if I strongly felt that I could bring something significant and fresh to it.

To me at least, coaching junior sport has been an exciting, enlightening, emotional and at times poignant journey with incredible highs and forgettable lows and a host of emphatically memorable characters, places and shared experiences to learn from, even if at times it all got a little out of hand. It had even returned a little romance into what was starting to feel like work. But it was all, nonetheless, an escape. And the time had come to return home and hang up the boots.

It took me a year.

Anfield 2000

Collective in chant, united
in contempt. The overpaid
below in new strips and sponsors
perform their silky acrobatics
for The Kop. It's not just abuse
that is hurled, but an almost personal
expectation that there, in the centre,
twenty million pounds away,
things must go according to song.
A scoreless draw may ensue.

But then that other game
played in surrounding streets,
where dignity sparkles
at the end of broken bottles
or festers at the far end
of a dole or ticket queue,
it gambols on with its own rules;
sweaty, angry, the close
of an eight-day week. Then
in an empty stadium, days later,

the air is electricity, full of ghosts.
We sit among them and soak in
an unswerving tradition of longing,
an insatiable desire to feel –
just for a millisecond –
a fleeting sense of victory.
Somewhere here the knowledge
you could not, you will not
ever walk alone
and never, truly, hopelessly lose.

4. Penalties:
Just a Game

So what I thought was, you can either break your heart trying to work it all out, or you can go and sit on a mountain.
– Salman Rushdie, *Midnight's Children*, 1981

In 1999, the team finished second, an almost healthy downer after the previous year's premiership joy. Despite this being, on paper, the strongest team I have ever coached, the balance between 'freedom and discipline' erred towards 'familiarity and indiscipline' and we blew our chance to make two-in-a-row premiership wins when we lost to the bottom-placed side, blaming the pitch, referee and global warming – anything but our own uncreative play. We were caught in the rut of routine which thankfully the trip to the UK seemed to repair.

In 2000, the boys returned to form, brimming with confidence and cohesion after the overseas escapade and carved up every team put in front of it at the Under 17 level. As for me? Well, I spent what was to be my final year of soccer coaching in a state of incredulity. Uninspired if not dulled by these great results and too little adversity, I began what could only be described as 'Pohwni-hunting', a deliberate and malevolent mental assassination of those I felt unworthy to have the privilege of being within a kilometre of sportschildren.

My telepathic venom essentially consisted of a mental swiping at morons as media-worthy as Damir Dokic or as blissfully silly as the coach of a bottom-placed club side in the Under 17s who spent the entire match (as well as pre-match, half-time and post-game diatribes) ranting at how uncommitted and undetermined a certain eleven individuals in his club's colours were. I could be wrong, but I think I detected a faint UK accent there, too. We beat them 8–1.

Once more, having a winning team was a pressure I was not used to. No longer the underdog, I found myself in the position of wanting to hold *myself* in contempt. And if I shot myself down, surely nobody could accuse me of arrogance. In all honesty, I was looking for reasons to quit. My team's great form in itself would be a great reason to stop – quit while you're ahead. If the lads won a third premiership – hell, I could do a Mal Meninga. I never ever would've thought that'd be possible in my lifetime.

And then that little devil dude returns, hops up on my shoulder and tells me, *There's more trophies where these came from* and *There's many more teams to obliterate and coaches to humiliate* and *Besides, your war against the pohwni is not yet over. Look at the evil around you...*

He was right.

A month back into the swing of things, a friend told me that his eight-year-old son's team had lost 9–0 on the weekend. They couldn't get their act together and – bless their little hearts – the tackers just threw in the towel after the fourth goal whizzed past their goalie. The coach's response next training – in, of course, his infinite wisdom – was to give the lads a good forty-five-minute jog in order to think about what big wimps they were. His son, a team member, was the biggest girl's blouse of the lot of them. A good ol' back-breaking run never did Pops any harm when he was a kid and possibly made him The Man He Is Now. And, in any case, it'd certainly improve the boys' stamina and give 'em close to a good hour to think about what big wimps they were.

In case you missed it, this was an Under 8 team we're talking about. I personally think 'Pops' needs a good forty-five-minute slap with a floppy rubber chicken.

I needed the poultry again the following weekend.

I had spent many months earlier in the year encouraging

a mute, insecure but lovable little 'outcast' to play soccer in a younger Radford team. I figured fresh air and working in a team was just what the doctor ordered. My gentle soft sell was showing signs of working (he ran away much more slowly) and, after getting him happily and successfully to participate in another rewarding romp of 'cowpat football' on Year 7 Camp, felt I was on a roll with Wilbur. I sent a registration form home via his reliable big sister (big sisters are always reliable) and, after asking only seven times for it to be completed and brought in to me, had it there on my desk the day before registrations closed. I sent it in with a satisfied smile.

During something like the third match of the season, a dangerously moronic pohwni – one of those mind bogglingly stupid cretins who run up and down the touchline yelling atrociously inane recommendations like *Stop being slack, will ya!?* or *Push up, defence!* while covering more miles of ground than any of the players on the field – went and wrecked everything. After a close loss, he asked the coach in his subtle, sensitive, booming voice, *Why the hell did you put on Wilbur? This is an important match and he was out of his league and let that forward get the winning goal. He cost the team the match, you know.* He seemed oblivious to the fact that Wilbur was standing within earshot. Wilbur, who was up until that point oblivious of the fact that he was solely to blame for the opposition's goal, pricked up his ears when he heard his name mentioned. His father and the coach had just praised him for giving his best, so he was really being noticed for once – more than usual.

Confused by the conflicting messages he was receiving – let's face it, he was confused enough already – he took the more convincing pohwni's booming oration of the truth as gospel – and unceremoniously quit.

Now, if I had in my possession the world's entire thermonuclear arsenal, I would have quite inauspiciously pointed them all at that bloke's head and unceremoniously pushed the little red button.

Days later, at a parent-teacher interview, a mother (who months earlier had been over the moon about her son's selection in a junior representative team) was bemoaning how she wished her kid had never made the squad: *He's lost his love of soccer, George. It's all so super-serious now. Their spots in the squad are always 'on the line' and they're all expected to be so adult in their training regime. It's all total discipline and total rigour. Drills, skills and more drills. Never about having fun. He wants to quit soccer altogether. And you know how much he loves it...*

She went on to describe a training session that sounded like something out of *Starship Troopers*. The more I listened, the angrier I got. Couldn't these coaches see that they were totally, rigorously and systematically killing a young boy's passion and love for the game? Is there anything worse you could do to a kid? Maybe get them to jog for forty-five minutes?

I'm pretty certain that representing your state and playing at the elite level is a big honour which comes at a high cost. I cannot disregard the crowning glory that these achievements bestow on those 'selected', but my arty-farty happy-hippie side seems to remind me constantly that kids are not supposed to be refining, perfecting and turning themselves into efficient machines in their early teens. They should be tasting, sampling and enjoying the many things on offer in childhood, making boo-boos along the way and sometimes be spared the burdens of responsibility which will inevitably come later in life.

Yep, that's almost my Dad talking.

I have seen so many young elite sportskids in my time 'identified' as being super-dooper at an early age. They then train nine days a week, filling in the spare hours with their school work and maybe finding precious seconds to spend some quality time with friends once every month or two. Sure, some of these make the Olympics, Wimbledon, World Cups or become the Superfish of the future. I would never deny that it is well worth it all for them. But most burn out and throw it all away along with their sweaty towels when they reach their senior school years. Then wonder where their childhood went.

A balance needed to be struck somewhere along the line.

A work colleague, Andrew Wrigley, once got me thinking about what exactly is meant by 'service to sport'. He postulated that, with sport becoming so unromantically success-oriented these days, at least with 'juniors', we need to think in terms of how *sport can serve our kids*. I concur. If all it serves is an anxiety burger with myopic sauce mixed in with a side order of unreasonable expectation, then I don't want a combo meal. Yet if it can serve young people the value of friendship, teamwork and learning – about themselves and the world – with a light sprinkling of fun, fitness and fresh air, then I want a Happy Meal. Bravo, Andrew!

Like my father, I could never make the sort of demands on kids which destabilise their sense of perspective and restrict the ownership of their own lives. *It's up to you.* You have to enjoy what it is that you do. Work hard, sure, but enjoy it. God, we're already too serious about sport and life as it is.

I recall on that night of the parent-teacher interview I saw on the television news that two Leeds United supporters were murdered in Turkey, where they went to support their side in a Cup Winners' Cup semi-final away leg against Galatassary (the eventual winners). *People die for this*, my father rightly said about war... and sport. Needless to say, the match went ahead as scheduled. After all, the show must go on.

It was all apparently worth more than two lives.

I pick up the paper today and read about a mayor in Den Bosch, The Netherlands, cancelling a game because a knife-wielding nutter, carried away by something other than a love or loyalty for the game and his club, was shot by police. Across the globe in Isidro Casanova, Buenos Aires, a teenager had died from wounds inflicted by rubber bullets during a confrontation between fans and police. And in England, Saturday night was definitely all right for fighting as three hundred rival soccer fans from the two Division 1 Sheffield teams (United and Wednes-day) went hammer and tongs in a downtown area after a local derby. Thirty-three morons were arrested, and riot gear, tear gas and batons were deployed. The match was a 1–1 draw.

I can remember the words that echoed through my head in two hospital waiting rooms, when I realised that nothing is all that important when compared to a life: *It's just a game.* Hold it all up on a higher plane. Compared to the planets, a soccer ball is a very microscopically small ball. Whichever way it rolls is hardly as crucial as the blips on a life support.

No. It's not worth more than a childhood. It's not worth more than an adolescence. It's not worth more than a life. Nowhere near it.

As it happened, my boys won another premiership in 2000, their third in five years. Although nothing is as good as the first time, the 2000 win was sweet, with the team remaining undefeated – a feat which we had not achieved in 1998 – and, as a result, winning the championship by fourteen points. Along with their Runners-Up medal in 1999 and a successful UK tour to boot, our journey together would have impressed even the greatest sceptics of half a decade ago.

I was lucky. My team had achieved everything I had dreamed about as a player and a coach. I was more than aware that their success was something very few people get a chance to experience in a lifetime. My team had now ironically become what I had initially loathed from a jealous distance: that slick, sporting, invincible spawn of Satan coached by the biggest, loneliest demon of 'em all: me.

Then again, maybe that's too harsh. Weren't we all just little boys with similar dreams and aspirations, some real determination, some natural talent and a desire to do our best and show others what we could do? Even with all the distractions and seductions of regular winning, it is a testament to the boys that they never really lost this boyish zest and wonder. After all, we certainly started as we finished: a bunch of pals enjoying our play together, needing to do a little work in two key areas – defence and attack.

As I lifted up the premiership trophy for a third time, I looked skyward and said, for the third time as well, *This one's for you, Dad.* I am sure, for a winning moment, I was the happiest person on the planet.

Before this match, I had watched the little Under 13 Division 2s down below on the lower paddock at Radford, happy in their own 'Minor Cup' victory – winning a subsidiary competition within their division's lower ranks – and felt an awful pang of déjà vu. Would I do it all again?

That's the problem. Sport can be so bloody insatiable.

Like a parent clutching a report card and demanding to know why you didn't get five As instead of four, it demands that you keep on proving and *im*proving what you are and what you can do. There'd be a whole new breed of thought-resistant pohwnis to contend with. And all that expectation. The little pipsqueaks

212

had asked me all year when I'd next take a team to England. I certainly didn't want to get caught in that wheel again, did I?

Should I quit?

Weeks later, the dust started to settle on the trophy cabinet, now blissfully full, Dad's face still emanating from the many heads beaming in the plethora of framed team photos that linger there with a one-armed trophy. Mum was packing a mini version of her Sideline Café for my silly upcoming camping trip. She was of the opinion that I should stay home and have a rest.

A day later, it was Dad's face I'd see once again, during a sublime moment, superimposed above the crooked smile of the horizon, there at the summit of Mt Exmouth in the beautiful Warrumbungles. I had made the seven-hour trip from Canberra with five willing members of my team – to ironically unwind and forget about match reports, team sheets and for'n'againsts.

The climb up Mt Exmouth was a bitch. The first section came easily – then some windy, horrid steep bits ensued before the ascent flattened momentarily, prior to a final, rocky uphill assault to the peak. After a few false crests, we made it to the top.

I sensed allegory.

As it had been nine months earlier when I found myself leaning over that turret at Warwick Castle, the view was intoxicatingly serene. There was hardly a cloud in the sky and you could see quite clearly for miles and miles and miles. As you spun around to capture the 360-degree view in one delectable panorama, you saw all the places we had previously hiked: The Breadknife, Belougery Spire, Crater Bluff and Bluff Mountain, and in the distance, Tonduran Spire standing alone and goofy, like a forgotten substitute waiting to go on. Then, turning south, the landscape evened out into lush, green and brown rectangles, through which a road curled portent-ously homeward.

I found my thoughts returning to my father and that beautiful moment seventeen years ago when I was these boys' age. Dad, leaning on the goalpost, and me so crusty and adolescent.

I think I might take some time out.

He nods. Inhales. Replies. *You can always come back to it.*

The troops stir. The memory is broken.

I want to remember this view, says Fattie. *Will you write a poem about it, H?*

214

Keysie was singing *I Can See For Miles and Miles* – now well and truly articulate in old folks' muzak; Matthew was recounting some lecture I'd given him once about getting perspective from higher altitudes; Blondie was perhaps considering where to put the rubber chicken for the next sequence of photographs; and Jimmy? He had that look of quiet satisfaction you get when you finish things off. Like a goal. Or a steep ascent.

I didn't have a mirror, but I was probably looking and feeling the same way.

The World Game

For Wim Jonk and Rory Kleeman

i.

Two losses this week,

a member of your family
and a match. And you said

it's only a game in the end, isn't it?
fiddling with your laces. I mean,
it's not like losing a loved one, is it?

The funeral gave no answers.
But your boots were in the car.
And you knew, if you hurried,
you would make it back by kick-off.

ii.

There are complaints of cramps,
decisions, fouls,
sprains –

as a funeral procession
of bruised egos
drags themselves off to the car park

followed closely behind,
                    like shadows,
                    by their children.

iii.

People die for this, father
            said about
            two things

and one was war

iv.

Dad was a cigarette man.

They were always there.
Like wrinkles.
And loss.

And between those tender lips
he'd suck away at
the thought –

not totally erased
by the Germans
way back on another, larger rectangle –
that he had some bearing on things.

v.

You are never more alive than when a game is in
motion.
That's what every player knows:
in every moment played –
of any match –
at any given time –
that –
that is the only moment
occurring
anywhere
in the world...
Mark my words.

You know it's true.

vi.

I'm a chewing gum man myself,

disposed to churn
and mull until
the taste

has long since disappeared.

vii.

Unlike poetry,
the only language

of the world game
is cliché:

We held our heads up
We lifted a notch
and took it to 'em

We won the 50-50 balls
more often than not –
we played all over 'em...

But the best side won on the day.

viii.
Well not entirely.

ix.

It's like you're pumping out
a sadness,

converting it to muscle
so that tomorrow

you'll be more resilient
in the mirror.

The tone
is slightly tensile

as the biceps bend
to lift an Umbro bag –

a white shirt dangling
from the open zipper.

Tonight you are staying at Dad's.

x.

In the theatre of dreams:
...a team of Umbro-black Gestapo is taking my Dad away
from the grounds and he's yelling, *It's only a game* as on
the field two crews of automatons, programmed only
to win, battle out a scoreless draw and across the other
sideline a coffin, linesman as pallbearers, is heading off
towards the dressing rooms to a slow national anthem
and there's tears in your eyes because you didn't
– *couldn't* – win the 50-50 ball and all I can repeat over
and over is *Hey, I told you, people die for this...*

xi.

I don't really know how you could play
with death still rippling, nagging

like a hamstring strain. *This
one's for him* I can hear you say,

and believe. But believe me, this game –
this clumsy cliche of losing and living –

it's played for the self, no less,
and all the rest is like some minor foul
                    without consequence.

Bibliography

Articles

Abjorensen, Norman. 'Looking For a Place Within', *Canberra Times*, 23 January 2001.

Doherty, Megan. 'Welcome to the Reign of George the Great', *Canberra Times*, 14 January 2001.

Hall, Matthew. 'World at Their Feet', *The Bulletin*, 13 June 2000

Sargent, Greg. 'General Tips for Mental Toughness Training', *Sports Coach*, Autumn 1988.

Webb, John. 'Doing Ourselves an Injury', from 'Men & Sport', in *XY: Men, Sex, Politics,* Spring 1995.

'Kids Opt for TV, Videos', *Canberra Times*, 19 January 2000

'Violence at Soccer Leaves Two Dead', *Canberra Times*, 19 December 2000.

Books

Astley, Thea. *Drylands*, Ringwood, Victoria: Penguin, 1999.

Bryson, Bill. *Down Under*, Sydney: Doubleday 2000.

Bryson, Bill. *Notes from a Big Country*, Sydney: Black Swan, 1998.

Daley, Laurie & Middleton, David. *Always a Winner*, Sydney: Harper Sports, 2000.

Drewe, Robert. *The Shark Net*, Ringwood, Victoria: Viking, 2000.

Earle, Robbie & Davies, Daniel. *One Love: The Reggae Boyz: An Incredible Soccer Journey*, London: Andre Deutsch, 1998.

Gekoski, Rick. *Staying Up*, London: Warner Books, 1998.

Rowling, J.K. *Harry Potter and the Philosopher's Stone*, London: Bloomsbury, 1997.

Rushdie, Salman. *The Ground Beneath Her Feet*, Sydney: Jonathan Cape, 1999.

Schiavello, Michael, ed. *A Century of Soccer: 100 Years of the World Game*, Mulgrave, Victoria: S&I Publishing, 1998.

Slater, Robbie & Hall, Matthew. *The Hard Way*, Sydney: Harper Sports, 1999.

Internet

Hawkes, Timothy F. 'Teaching Social Responsibility', apapdc online conference, 2000, available from http://www. apapdc.cdu.au/conference2000/papers/art_2_12.htm, accessed 2 February 2001.

'The White Horses', Wiltshire Web: Historical Wiltshire, available from http://www.wiltshire-web.co.uk/history/horse.htm, accessed 24 December 2000.

Video

Benigni, Roberto. *Life is Beautiful*, 1997.

Bragg, Melvyn. Sam Mendes Interview, 1999.

Coerver Coaching. *The Creative Dribbler*, Coerver Products, 1996.

Acknowledgements

At the start of his memoir *The Twelfth of Never*, Louis Nowra states that

> some of the names in this book have been changed and sometimes the chronology isn't as exact as it should be, and I am sure others might disagree with my memories of certain events.'

I couldn't put it better myself.

I would like to thank more than anyone else my incomparable and indefatigable researcher Bruce Coe. There is no more meticulous and generous-natured sports-lover on the planet.

I would also like to acknowledge the efforts of Fi Atkin, Jerry Hearn, Daniel Maloney, Arran McKenna, Belinda Pearson and Andrew Wrigley for helpful comment and encouragement at the early stages of this book; Theo Huitker and Steven Hablous for international facts and figures and sending me the video *Het Succes van 88* respectively; Rory Kleeman for finding that elusive Gordon Strachan quote; Justin Brown for sending me the immortal words of Robert Waisege and Margaret Wente; Dylan Mordike and Problem Child Productions for clearing up the image; Susan Glenn-Hume for the stuff on men in sport; Nick Guoth for facts on the Canberra Arrows; Barbara Coe for editorial advice; Sally Mordike for the definitive once-over; Kelly Elliott for presidency of the Canadian branch of the Radford First XI Fan Club; my publisher Stephen Matthews for helping me define what it is to be a man of the new millennium; and the reflections and reminiscences of many players.

Thanks also to Robert de Castella and Les Murray (SBS) for their 'big-name' endorsements of this book and the confidence which their words gave me; Dick Telford and my favourite soccer Olyroo Jack Lennard (of '56) for saying such nice things at the launch; the Radford Bill Turner squad of 2001 for helping me to experience how a Dutch national coach feels during 'penalties', while simultaneously nagging me to write about them in *Not Just Footy II*; and Chris Conti and Danny Moulis for their support with acquittal references.

The majority of the photographs were taken by Bruce Coe, John Fraser and Vince Sutherland.

The writing of this book was assisted by artsACT

'An intractable phenomenon of writing an auto-biography is that you begin to miss the people you are writing about.'

– John Irving, *The Imaginary Girlfriend, A Memoir*, 1996

Genoeg is genoeg.

As a kid, George Huitker played representative baseball nd tennis without having a parent on either junior sport's governing boards. He also attempted little athletics, cricket, indoor soccer, judo, jujitsu, netball, soccer, softball and touch football – but an impetuous nature meant a failure in most of these sporting experiments. He has coached both indoor and outdoor soccer – the sport that he has persisted with – for over fifteen years.

Huitker is often seen in attendance at Presentation Nights for soccer, theatre and poetry – three hobbies which also happen to be intrinsically linked to his job as a schoolteacher at Radford College, Canberra, where he has taught Drama (and even English) and quite dramatically coached indoor and outdoor football (and even softball) at various times since 1989.

He has formed various theatre companies over the years, finally settling with his own independent theatre company, Huitker Movement Theatre (HMT) in 2002. HMT received funding from artsACT for its inaugural season and has since gone on to win many local industry awards for its productions which regularly attract quality directors, actors and discerning audiences. His 2001 memoir *Not Just Footy*, published by Ginninderra Press, was adapted for the stage in 2004 by HMT under the watchful eye of Canadian director Walter Learning and played to packed houses. He has also published a collected work of poetry entitled *An Unfamiliar Actor* (2002) also with Ginninderra Press.

About to enter the forties, Huitker recently revived his Touch Football playing career with The Power, a multi-aged, all sizes sporting collective. He provided the team with much comic relief while they provided him with a premiership trophy after three years and 58 games of essentially annoying teams of a much older average age.

Huitker is perhaps most proud of his recent efforts to link sport with charity through his teamSUPPORT initiative, an exciting venture which will feature (alongside The Power) in his new book *Little Life*, the final instalment in the Not Just Footy trilogy.

Visit notjustfootyclub.com.au right now!

Praise for *How To Succeed Without Really Winning*:

First-rate, original, distinguished by a congenial tone throughout. Includes an outstanding bibliography. If only we could all be so lucky as to have had George Huitker for a coach.

2006 ACT Writing & Publishing Awards Citation

If Bill Shankly's famous 'life and death' credo was about the destination, then Huitker's yarn is about the journey. The sequel to *Not Just Footy* continues the Canberra teacher, writer and football buff's coaching odyssey through the wild landscape of junior sport. It is one of the infinite intersections where stakeholders have the choice of embracing the inherent beauty and life-enforcing ways of the contest, or heading down the path to boorish beahviour and madness - a narrow tract between balance and obsession. Funny, tragic and richly sourced, it is not just a must-read for anyone like Uday Hussein, but all of us who've been temporarily unhinged by our sporting passions.

Neil Jameson – *Inside Sport*

The author's *leitmotiv* is that a win-at-all-costs attitude is positively harmful. As Huitker puts it, 'You can genuinely grow, develop and succeed through loss.' It seems to me that there is so much practical wisdom in this book that it should be required reading for all those involved in the vital task of coaching and supervising children's sport.

J Neville Turner – *Sporting Traditions*

In *How To Succeed Without Really Winning* George Huitker has truly given us a gift. He has taken the time to reflect on our tendency to invest so much in the outcome of a 'measly game' of junior sport that the behaviour of adults – coaches, managers, parents and supporters – leaves much to be desired. This book should be required reading for everyone involved in junior sport, much the way that coaches are required to sign a Code of Ethics. A copy should be shared among the associates of every team! If the book is used as a guide, even once, it will have saved some juniors from the horrors most of us remember only too well.

Rae Wells – *Sports Coach*

Many sports, such as cricket, have – until recently, anyway – stressed that 'the game's the thing', and that the result should be secondary. But what's different about Huitker's book is its presentation, drawing on a frame of reference from Shakespeare to the Dalai Lama to lyrics from the pop group Kiss. In fact, in its gently didactic style, the book is reminiscent of Alain de Botton's *The Consolations of Philosophy* set in a sporting context.

Philip O'Brien – *The Canberra Times*